WOMEN MENTORING WOMEN

UPDATED

WOMEN MENTORING WOMEN

*Ways to Start,
Maintain,
and Expand
a Biblical
Women's
Ministry*

VICKIE KRAFT
AND GWYNNE JOHNSON

MOODY PUBLISHERS
CHICAGO

First Edition
© 1992 by
VICKIE KRAFT

Revised Edition
© 2003 by
VICKIE KRAFT and GWYNNE JOHNSON

All Scripture quotations, unless otherwise indicated, are taken from the *Holy Bible, New International Version*®. NIV®. Copyright © 1973, 1978, 1984 by International Bible Society. Used by permission of Zondervan Publishing House. All rights reserved.

Scripture quotations marked AMP are taken from the *Amplified Bible, Old Testament,* copyright © 1965, 1987 by The Zondervan Corporation. The *Amplified New Testament, New Testament,* copyright © 1954, 1958, 1987 by The Lockman Foundation. Used by permission.

Library of Congress Cataloging-in-Publication Data

Kraft, Vickie, 1928-
   Women mentoring women: ways to start, maintain, and expand a biblical women's ministry / Vickie Kraft,
Gwynne Johnson.--Rev. ed.
      p. cm.
   ISBN 0-8024-4889-5
   1. Church work with women. 2. Women--Religious life. I. Johnson, Gwynne, 1938- II. Title.
BV4445 .K73 2003
253'.082--dc21
                                                                                              2002012770

3 5 7 9 10 8 6 4 2

Printed in the United States of America

*To all the godly women who have encouraged me
and invested their lives in mine,
beginning with my mother*

CONTENTS

Part 4 Cultivating the Garden

Part 5 Gathering a Bouquet of Flowers

Part 6 An Almanac of Resources

ACKNOWLEDGMENTS

This book is not the work of one woman. It is tangible evidence of what women can do when they work together in harmony and love. The 1990–91 Women's Ministries Board in Northwest Bible Church worked with dedication to host a seminar, "Building an Effective Women's Ministry." The manual they prepared for that seminar was the seedbed for this workbook.

Hundreds of other women have my gratitude for selflessly giving of their time and energy to make the Women's Ministries Program at Northwest Bible Church a blessing.

I want to especially thank Gayle Davidson, who encouraged me to complete this book.

Finally, Gwynne Johnson has my deep gratitude for her organizing and editing skills and for applying to this project the insight she has gained from her own experience in ministering to women.

We pray that God will use this book to encourage and enable churches to prepare Women's Ministries Programs that will bring their women to spiritual maturity and equip them to serve in their church and community wherever there is a need.

Our goal is that the Lord Jesus Christ be glorified in the lives of Christian women everywhere.

FOREWORD TO
THE 2003 EDITION

The twenty-first century has brought new urgency for Christian women to wrap their faith in meaningful relationships because <u>our increasingly secular lifestyle isolates and discourages women.</u> <u>The presence of women in the workplace has radically changed marriage and family life</u>. Medical advances have lengthened lives and complicated health management. <u>Emotional crises have multiplied, and intense spiritual needs are often overlooked. The need of women for each other has never been greater</u>.

Every survey of women emphasizes a feeling of pressure and entrapment, even among Christians. But <u>the woman who knows how to access God's peace will weather her personal storms</u>. She navigates through life with her Pilot, Jesus Christ, who knows how to calm rough seas. Just as He commanded the storm in Galilee, "Peace, be still," so He knows how to quiet her soul. And He invites her to bring her sisters on board.

Until the mid-twentieth century, organized Women's Ministries were sporadic and restricted, but today, thanks to our economy and technology, women are now largely free to join groups and <u>find female companionship</u>. Committed followers of Christ have always sought to share His love and joy with others, and Vickie Kraft is such a person. She and her husband, Fred, were well known as capable leaders of children's ministries, but one day over a cup of coffee she shared with my husband and me her fervor to obey God's command in Titus 2: "<u>Teach the older women. . . . Then they can train the younger women</u>." Shortly thereafter we rejoiced to see Vickie and Fred launch a fledgling ministry called Titus 2:4 Ministries, and it is from that seed plot that this book has grown.

These biblical roots are trustworthy; the book of Titus was Paul's directive to his young protégé who struggled in a godless, depraved society on the island of Crete. God's ingenious method for upgrading women placed responsibility on older women from whom life-changing attitudes and conduct must be learned. Cultural improvements start in the home, and they begin in the hearts of the world's most powerful influencers—homemakers.

Thoroughly biblical and intensely practical, *Women Mentoring Women* offers the solution to a chronic weakness in churches, namely, involvement of well-balanced, well-taught functioning wives, sisters, mothers, and daughters, from blossoming gen-X-ers to senior grannies. Vickie is a gifted and caring teacher who writes out of years of training and experience. As I travel with my husband, Howard, many women tell me they cannot come to terms with their femaleness in one way or another. Many feel alone in their faith and long for role models and helping hands. Here is a wise biblical rationale, a how-to plan that enables women to knit together the fraying fabric of our society.

A portable gold mine, this book belongs in every church library and on the shelf of every leader of Women's Ministry. If they know how, women can do the salvage job with other women. As never before we should be "making the most of every opportunity because the days are evil" (Ephesians 5:16).

Jeanne Hendricks

INTRODUCTION

Over the past ten years since the first printing of *Women Mentoring Women,* women's responses confirm our biblical conviction that women need women for emotional health and spiritual growth. Churches of many traditions all over America began or strengthened Women's Ministries Programs using this book as a reference and guide.

Internationally the book has been translated into at least ten languages, evidence that women's impact on women is not simply an American idea suited only for this culture. Women in Latin America, Europe, Asia, Russia, and the Middle East have welcomed and used the concepts provided here, creatively adapting them to their culture and differing resources.

The original interview made with James Dobson of Focus on the Family first aired in 1992. Since then it has been re-aired three additional times, and each broadcast stimulates new inquiries.

Since 1992, many more churches are now hiring women for their staff to direct the Women's Ministry. Not only has this benefited all the women of the church, but it has proved to be an asset to the male staff as well. When a woman on staff is available to be included in the decision-making process, the concerns of women of the congregation are discussed at the early, planning stage of ministry. A staff woman also brings the advantages of her uniquely feminine viewpoint into such discussions. My experience as the Minister to Women for a metropolitan church with a large staff for over thirteen years confirmed this.

Today, ten years after our first publication date, seminaries are recognizing the need to educate and train women for these staff positions. Consequently, several seminaries now include in their curriculum a Women's Ministry Track and some even offer a Doctor of Ministry degree in Women's Ministry.

It has been very encouraging personally to see God use this book and those written by others to affirm to women God's view of their value and His expectations. He has charged us with the responsibility to serve Him as role models and mentors of the generations following us. We are to encourage and equip them to live for God's glory. If we don't shoulder this responsibility, that job won't be done, because no one can model godly womanhood except a woman who lives to please God. That makes our participation in His program vital to the future of the church.

Titus 2:4 Ministries, Inc., the ministry which I co-founded with my husband in 1984, continues to challenge women to see their responsibility to be involved in God's purpose for their lives. This ministry includes speaking engagements, retreats, conferences, and consulting. For further information we can be contacted at:

Titus 2:4 Ministries, Inc.
P. O. Box 797566
Dallas, TX 75379-7566
972-447-0252
Titus24women@aol.com
www.titus2-4.org

Vickie Kraft

Part One

THE SEED:
THE WORD OF GOD

The grass withers and the flowers fall,
but the word of our God stands forever.

ISAIAH 40:8

One

QUALIFIED
FOR MINISTRY

As children, many of us experienced the thrill of burying a tiny seed in a Styrofoam cup and keeping daily vigil until a tentative green sprout nudged the dirt aside, unfolded, and became our own small plant. Whether it ever arrived at full maturity or not, the growing plant was reflective of whatever seed we planted: from a tomato seed, a tomato; from a flower seed, a flower; from a green bean seed, a bean plant. The future product was bound up in the seed. In much the same way, the end result in any women's ministry will depend largely upon the kind of planted seed, the source of our presuppositions and our activities.

As we look to the Bible as the seed for our planting, we can confidently expect that the result will be a ministry that reflects God's character and God's view of women. Therefore, the place to begin growing your women's ministry is with a study of what the Bible teaches about women and their responsibilities before God. This study is vital for several reasons.

Tradition Versus Truth

First, we need to distinguish between tradition and biblical truth. There is a difference between tradition and Scripture. The Bible is divine and infallible; tradition is human and fallible. When tradition is based partially on Scripture and partially on culture, we must distinguish where one begins and the other ends. Discerning the impact of culture and tradition on the understanding of truth is important in planning how to implement this essential ministry to women. The seed thoughts for any effective and lasting ministry must come from the Word of God.

Biblical Calling or Cultural Pressure?

Second, social and cultural changes, such as a pervasive immorality, an increasing divorce rate, the breakdown of the extended family, and an increase in the number of mothers working outside the home, have created an atmosphere of confusion and unrest experienced by many women today, including Christian women. However, when we are pressured to develop a program centered on the needs of women in our culture rather than beginning with what the Bible teaches, we are in danger of developing a ministry with culture-bound roots. The Bible, rightly understood and applied, will provide a program that speaks with authority and power to the needs of women.

Commands or Confusion?

Third, many women are hesitant to step into a significant role of ministry because they honestly believe it is not their place to do so. They have previously understood that the Bible places great restrictions on their ministry in the church, and they sincerely desire to be obedient to God's plan. They need the strong confidence of scriptural clarity to step out.

In this chapter we will examine the biblical basis for a woman's worth and God's place for her in ministry from the perspective of women as *qualified* for ministry. In the next chapter we will discuss women as *called* to ministry.

Qualified by Original Design

One of the first things the Bible tells us about women is that they have been created in the image of God.

Then God said, "Let us make man in our image, in our likeness, and let them rule over the fish of the sea and the birds of the air, over the livestock, over all the earth, and over all the creatures that move along the ground."

So God created man in his own image,
in the image of God he created him;
male and female he created them.

God blessed them and said to them, "Be fruitful and increase in number; fill the earth and subdue it. Rule over the fish of the sea and the birds of the air and over every living creature that moves on the ground."... And it was so. God saw all that he had made, and it was very good. (Genesis 1:26–31)

Man and woman were created *equal in nature.* They are persons of intellect, emotions, volition, and spirit. God also assigned them joint responsibility and personal accountability. They were both given dominion; the woman was co-regent with her husband. They were mutually blessed; together they were to reproduce. Neither one could have done it alone, so it was a joint blessing.

However, although created to be *equal in nature,* they were also created *different in source and in function.* Adam was created from the dust of the ground, but the woman was created from him, from a rib taken from his side (Genesis 2:21–23). Therefore, they had a different source. Their physical bodies were different, and their function in reproduction was different. Both were essential.

Not only that, but the woman is said to have a *different purpose.* She was created to be a "helper suitable to him." The word *helper* has often been misunderstood today. Some have taken it to mean a doormat, an inferior person. Interestingly, the Hebrew word translated "helper" (*ezer*) is used nineteen times in the Old Testament (for example, Exodus 18:4; Deuteronomy 33:7; Psalms 10:14; 33:20). Only four times is it used to speak of people helping people, peer helping peer. The other fifteen times it is used to refer to God helping people, a superior helping an inferior. It is *never* used in any of the nineteen references of an inferior helping a superior. The term also has the meaning of someone who brings another to fulfillment.

Eve could be a "helper suitable for" Adam because she was his equal in personhood. God brought all the animals before Adam first to demonstrate that not one there was for him. He needed someone like himself. And he recognized her, exclaiming in essence, "Wow! This is now bone of my bones and flesh of my flesh." This was what he had been waiting for. She could complete him because she was his equal in personhood. Yet because Adam and Eve were different from one another, each supplied what the other one lacked.

God instituted marriage for the protection of our sexuality. Physical intimacy is one of God's richest gifts, given with love to be fully enjoyed within the protective fence of marriage, between one woman and one man. Throughout the Bible, sexuality within marriage is honored, valued, and celebrated; however, sexual relationships outside of marriage are consistently condemned. Marriage is the fence a loving God established for the protection of His people.

Man's Designer and Creator knows best how we were designed to function as His creatures. God's image is man, male and female, created equals, to be in perfect harmony with one another and with their Creator. Man and woman were to function as His representatives on earth. They were to share equally in everything: in obedience, in blessing, in ruling and subduing, in reproducing, and in fellowshiping with God in the garden.

Therefore, the first reason that woman can enjoy a sense of worth is that she was created in God's image. She is qualified for ministry through creation.

Qualified by Redemption

The second reason the Christian woman can enjoy a healthy sense of self-worth and feel confident to minister is that she was redeemed at great price. Even today, we often determine the value of an item from the price paid for it. Think of the recent sale in the millions of dollars for one painting by Picasso. How much more valuable are those who have been redeemed at the greatest price, the precious blood of Jesus Christ, the very Son of Almighty God. "For you know that it was not with perishable things such as silver or gold that you were redeemed from the empty way of life handed down to you from your forefathers, but with the precious blood of Christ, a lamb without blemish or defect" (1 Peter 1:18–19). "For Christ died for sins once for all, the righteous for the unrighteous, to bring you to God. He was put to death in the body but made alive by the Spirit" (3:18).

Galatians 3:28 says, "There is neither Jew nor Greek, slave nor free, male nor female, for you are all one in Christ Jesus." There is equality in Christ. With Him, no superiority or inferiority based on race, social class, or gender exists.

The way of salvation is the same for man and for woman. Each is a sinner. Each must personally trust Jesus Christ alone to save. Each is then forgiven, receives eternal life, becomes an adult son or daughter in God's family (Romans 8:16–17; Galatians 4:6–7), and becomes a priest with full access to God (1 Peter 2:9).

With salvation, the Holy Spirit comes to indwell each individual (1 Corinthians 6:19) and to give each one spiritual gifts without discrimination based on gender (1 Corinthians 12:7). Each person, man or woman, is responsible to live a life of dependence upon the Holy Spirit and obedience to the Lord.

A woman is qualified and equipped by redemption.

Qualified by Old Testament Example

A third reason women are qualified for ministry is that in Scripture God uses women in key ministry for Him. Abraham's wife Sarah is given as a model to follow in relationship to our own husbands (1 Peter 3:1–6). Her respect and response to Abraham reflect godly submission. But Sarah was no doormat. She was outspoken and feisty, yet protective and supportive of Abraham. However, it is interesting to note in

Genesis 21:12 that God commands Abraham to obey Sarah. Most women will admit they would enjoy having a voice from heaven say to their husbands, "Do whatever she tells you to do." That is what God did for Sarah. The same Hebrew word used for obeying God in Genesis 22:18 regarding Abraham's obedience to God is used in 21:12 concerning Abraham's obeying Sarah's words regarding Hagar.

Miriam, the sister of Moses, is called a prophetess (Exodus 15:20–21), one who speaks God's word; and in Micah 6:4 God tells Israel that He set before them as leaders Moses, Aaron, *and* Miriam. In the latter passage, Miriam is clearly called one of the leaders of Israel.

Women the Bible calls "skilled" and "willing" voluntarily contributed of their possessions and worked with their hands in constructing the tabernacle (Exodus 35:21–22, 25–26). Women served in the doorway of the tabernacle. The same word for service was used of them as for the Levites (Exodus 38:8; 1 Samuel 2:22).

Most of us remember Deborah as the one who commanded Barak to lead the army when he was unwilling to step forward into leadership. But she was also a judge of Israel and a prophetess. She lived between Ramah and Bethel in Mount Ephraim, and the children of Israel came to her for judgment. In addition, following the great victory over Sisera, she demonstrated a poetic gift as she and Barak worshiped God in a song of praise (Judges 4–5). Her words are recorded for posterity.

Hannah was a woman of total commitment to and passion for God. She had access to God, made a vow, and kept it. Her deep faith and commitment gave Israel the prophet Samuel, a leader who turned the nation around, introduced the kingdom, and anointed Israel's first two kings (1 Samuel 9:16).

Abigail rescued her household by demonstrating great courage and initiative. She gave David wise counsel, calling him back to himself and to God, thereby saving him from taking murderous revenge (1 Samuel 25).

After the great conviction that ensued upon the reading of the Law, Josiah sent the high priest Hilkiah and his other officials to inquire of the Lord for him concerning what to do, since Israel had so long neglected God's word. Hilkiah went to Huldah, the prophetess, for God's directions, even though both Jeremiah and Zephaniah, also prophets of the Lord, were living in Jerusalem at the same time (2 Kings 22:11–20). It has sometimes been taught that women can do certain jobs only if there are no men available. This passage does not support that assertion.

The entire book of Esther recounts the story of a courageous young woman who risked her life and comfortable position to save her people from a murderous enemy. Her words "If I perish, I perish" are understood by all women who risk obedience to God in perplexing and difficult situations.

Proverbs 31 describes a woman who is often overwhelming to women who consider all that is written about her. Here was a priceless woman who feared God, cared for her family, managed her home, and used all her abilities and talents. She bought and sold land, manufactured and retailed textiles, and more. The scope of her activities was almost without limit. We can gain courage, however, when we consider that most likely this list covers a lifetime of effort, with no doubt different emphases in different seasons of her life—and she had servants to assist her. Certainly we can be encouraged if we look at the freedom, authority, and scope that lay open to her. She is praised for her exemplary life, not only by her children but also by her husband.

Women in the Old Testament were provided for in the ceremonial, civil, and moral law. They participated in worship, art, family life, and community life with creativity, decisiveness, freedom, and authority. They used their gifts and talents to serve God and to influence their families and their nation. It is important to realize that they were never forbidden to speak in public in the Old Testament.

Qualified by the Example of Jesus

Even in His agony on the cross, one of Jesus' last concerns was to provide for His mother's care. His attitude toward women was definitely countercultural. In a day when the rabbis said they would rather teach a dog than teach a woman and would rather burn the Torah than teach it to a woman, Jesus taught women spiritual truth (Luke 10:38–41; John 4; 11:1–44). He spoke to women publicly (John 4) when, by contrast, a rabbi would not even speak publicly to his wife. It was women who supported Jesus from their private wealth. It is also interesting to realize that Jesus let women travel with Him during His public ministry (Matthew 27:55; Luke 8:1–3).

Although women were not considered reliable witnesses in a legal matter, Jesus considered them to be valid witnesses (Luke 24:9–11). Indeed, it was to women that He gave the responsibility of being the first to testify to His resurrection. Many of Jesus' parables and illustrations contain examples with which women would particularly identify: the lost coin (15:8–10), yeast and bread (13:20–21), childbirth and labor (John 16:21). Jesus demonstrated unusual sensitivity and compassion toward women and performed miracles for them. He healed their sick and raised their dead to life (Luke 4:38–39; 8:40–56; 13:10–17; John 11:1–44). Rather than condemning them for even flagrant sexual sin, He forgave them and offered them new life (John 4:1–42; 8:1–11).

Mary's extravagant worship near His death was accepted by Jesus, and He defended her against the unjust criticism of the disciples (Mark 14:1–9; John 12:1–8). He guaranteed her remembrance in history for her love and generosity. His commendation, "She has done a beautiful thing to me. . . . She did what she could" (Mark 14:6, 8), provides insight into how God considers our talents, limitations, and opportunities when He gives us our final report card.

There is also an interesting balance between the sexes in the Gospel accounts. Both Mary the mother of Jesus and Zacharias the father of John the Baptist have a song that is recorded. In the temple, Simeon and Anna both welcomed the new baby. Jesus had conversations about the new birth with both Nicodemus and the Samaritan woman. Peter's confession, "You are the Christ, the Son of the living God" (Matthew 16:16), is balanced by Martha's similar confession in John 11:27. Both a man (Luke 6:6–10) and a woman (13:10–13) were healed in the synagogue; Jesus healed both a son and a daughter and raised a son and a daughter from the dead; and, as we have said, both men and women traveled with Jesus. This amazing balance is even more striking when the culture of Jesus' day is considered.

Jesus never spoke condescendingly to women, never made derogatory jokes about women, never humiliated or exploited women. No wonder they loved Him! Moreover, women did not deny, betray, or desert Him. They were last at the cross and first at the tomb, and after the Resurrection He appeared first to a woman, Mary Magdalene.

Qualified by the Example of the Early Church

What about women in the early church? Can we find historical precedent for a ministry by women? We can indeed. Women were present at Pentecost (Acts 2:1–4; cf. 1:12–14). Like Lydia and Priscilla, many hosted the early church meetings. There were no church buildings until the third century, and therefore all the early church meetings were conducted in homes. We can be sure that if women had not been involved, those homes would not have been available.

Women were active in ministry in the early church. In Acts alone, thirty-three women are named specifically. Priscilla was a teacher who taught Apollos. She and her husband, Aquila, were an effective team in the support and spread of the gospel. Paul calls her a "fellow worker" in Romans 16 and says that she and her husband risked their lives for him. Lydia, in Acts 16, was the first convert in Europe and hosted the church at Philippi. Dorcas was called a disciple, a helper of widows and the poor and someone who used her homemaking skills (Acts 9). Philip's four daughters were prophetesses (21:8–9). A prophet speaks God's word. Is it reasonable to believe that Philip's daughters were given the gift of prophecy and then forbidden to speak? It wouldn't make sense.

Euodia and Syntyche were women who "contended" at Paul's side for the gospel (Philippians 4:2–3). They were very influential in the church at Philippi and had a valuable ministry with Paul, something rarely noted because the reference in Philippians deals with a difficulty between these two women.

In Romans 16 ten women are mentioned, eight by name, and others are included in general phrases, such as "the household of Stephanos." Junias (feminine gender name) was a relative of Paul's whom he called "outstanding among the apostles" (v. 7). Like Stephen, in the Greek text Phoebe was called a *diakonos,* which translated means "servant," "minister," or "deacon." Furthermore, church history indicates that the early church had an order of women deacons who instructed women and prepared them for baptism. It was also recorded in Roman history that Christian women called "ministers" were imprisoned for their faith.

Phoebe is also called a *prostatis,* a Greek term meaning "patron," "protector," or "champion." This is the only place in the New Testament where this word is used. It is likely that she was like prominent Christian women today who sponsor significant projects for missions and outreach or who network to put those seeking to promote evangelism in touch with other significant people. She would pave the way with introductions.

In Romans 16 Paul refers to Mary, Tryphena, Tryphosa, and Persis in terms he does not use for the men. He states of the women that they all worked "hard in the Lord" (vv. 6, 12), an expression that in the Greek has the meaning of "toiling to the point of exhaustion."

Then Paul refers to Rufus's mother, "who has been a mother to me" (v. 13). How interesting to observe that Paul appreciated having a mother, just as anyone else. He never reached the point where he didn't enjoy having someone mother him a little.

Women were active in public worship. Often in reading 1 Corinthians 11 regarding women and head coverings, we become so involved in the head covering and what it is supposed to be that we forget the first words of verse 5, "And every woman who prays or prophesies." These women were speaking God's word and praying in the public worship service. Women were considered qualified and were given the opportunity to minister in the early church.

Qualified by Scriptural Injunction

What about Women's Ministries today? In 1 Corinthians 12 we see that each woman receives spiritual gifts for the building up of the body, not just for herself. The gifts are given by the Holy Spirit as He chooses without discrimination based on gender. Take, for instance, the gift of pastoring. In the Greek, "pastor" is the word *shepherd.* I believe there is a difference between the office and the gift, and that whereas there should be male leadership in the *office* of pastor, more women have the *gift* of pastoring than men. What is pastoring? It is feeding, caring for, and nurturing the sheep, and binding their wounds. What does that sound like? Mothering!

Ephesians 4:11–12 tells us that gifted people are given to the church to prepare God's people for works of service. Therefore, women are to be prepared and are to prepare others for service. Titus 2:3–5 teaches us clearly that the leadership of the church is to delegate to older, spiritually mature women the task of teaching and training the younger women in some specific ways.

In our churches today we have a great variety of ministries that are not specifically required by Scripture. But in Scripture there is a clear command for a ministry by women to women.

Qualified by Opportunity

There is almost no limit to what women can do today. They can evangelize, teach, serve on church staffs and committees, and be administrators. They can be involved in education at every level, from preschool to graduate school; in children's and youth ministries; in music, art, and drama. They can help the poor and needy in practical ways. Most of all, women can encourage women in this complex and confused society.

Women understand women. We must teach them the Word so that they know God's standards in order to be equipped for ministry. Then we must encourage them to use their gifts to serve each other and the world around them. It is essential to have women teachers and role models for the generation following us. We must examine our beliefs and attitudes about women and be certain that they are biblical rather than traditional or cultural. Men and women need one another, and neither can serve the Lord effectively with an attitude of independence, superiority, or inferiority toward the other.

In the Lord, however, woman is not independent of man, nor is man independent of woman. (1 Corinthians 11:11)

The Scripture passages given in this chapter should encourage you as you develop your Women's Ministry. Not only are you doing a job that God commands you to do, but also you are doing a job He has equipped you for. He has given you the resources you need to accomplish His work. You have His indwelling Spirit, who has gifted you and will enable you. You have the acceptance and love of the Son of God demonstrated to you in the Scriptures. You will have other gifted women to work with you, sharing your vision and ministry. Knowing when you set out that it is clearly God's will to develop a ministry for women to women will give you stability, certainty, and confidence. You will be able to stand firm and press onward regardless of obstacles.

Qualified by the Blessing Their Ministry Brings to the Entire Church

Jill Briscoe has well said about the need for women to have significant ministry, "When men of God recognize the gifts of women of God, and with their blessing and under their authority, encourage their use, the church of God will be blessed."

Women, both *single and married,* are blessed by a Women's Ministry because it helps them to mature spiritually. This maturing will affect every part of their lives. They will grow in confidence because they will learn that their self-worth is not derived from any human being but from God. Women working outside the home will see their employment as ministry. Single women will learn that they have value and opportunities for ministry. God loves us, as women. He will be a Father and husband to us (Psalm 68:5; Isaiah 54:5). He will give us an eternal impact as we serve Him.

The *family* is blessed as women become better wives and mothers, content with their influential responsibility to raise the next generation. Many husbands will be encouraged by the example of their wives to become more committed to the Lord. Marriages are strengthened.

The *church* is blessed by the involvement of these gifted women. Their participation will supply many more volunteers for service in every area. The image of God is male and female. The body of Christ is male and female. Therefore, this image should be reflected wherever possible. Women should be on the church staff, the worship committee, the missions board, the building committee, the mercies committee, the discipline committee, and the Christian education committee; and they should be involved teaching Sunday school and club programs.

Let me share with you some comments I've received from those who serve on the Women's Ministries Board of Northwest Bible Church about the benefits they have received from the women's ministry:

- "I now have strong relationships with other women I may not have met otherwise."
- "I feel so much more a part of our church."
- "My walk with the Lord has been strengthened by the role models of more mature women."
- "The opportunity to work with other women in a true team effort has been wonderful."
- "I love being accountable to the other women on the board."
- "I've developed skills in organization, leadership, and compromise."
- "I love the creativity and the brainstorming."
- "There is such a sense of family."
- "I've learned different approaches to problems."
- "My faith has been encouraged as I've seen God answer prayer."
- "Personally, I have become much more confident in my gifts and abilities, and I feel a great sense of accomplishment in what God has enabled me to do."

> - "I have become more comfortable in speaking before a group. I'm more sensitive to reaching out to newcomers and relating to people in general."
> - "The fellowship among the board members and the sharing of our lives has strengthened my female identity and heightened my self-esteem and self-acceptance. I feel more comfortable about allowing my imperfections to show, to drop my mask, to make mistakes. The years have shown me in a practical way that I am important because I'm me, not just because of what I do."

Wouldn't you agree that this is an essential ministry for every church? Nothing else can accomplish what an effective ministry to women by women will do. Male leaders in the home and church should not think of themselves as prison wardens whose job it is to confine and repress women. Instead, enlightened church leadership, like a husband who lovingly leads his family, should provide an atmosphere like a greenhouse. There women can grow, blossom, and develop to their full potential with the blessing, provision, protection, and encouragement of the church leadership.

Each woman is unique—there is no one exactly like you or me in all the world. Each of us is influential in the sphere God has given to us in which to make an impact on our family, church, place of employment, and friends. For that reason, each of us is responsible and accountable to God for how we use the gifts and opportunities He has given us. Each of us will stand before Him individually as a woman.

This is the message I hope you will bring to the women of your church. When you can demonstrate from Scripture how God values them and they begin to serve Him with enthusiasm and growing freedom, there is no limit to what can happen as God works through them in your congregation.

Questions for Study and Discussion

* * * * * * * * * * * *

1. Read Genesis 1:26–31. What do men and women share as persons created in the image of God?

2. Reach Genesis 2:18–25; Exodus 18:4; Deuteronomy 33:7; and Psalms 10:14; 33:20. From these passages, what do you learn about the word helper as used in Genesis 2:18, 20? Were any of these thoughts new to you?

3. Read Genesis 2:21–25. When was marriage instituted? What do you think is implied by the sentence "The man and his wife were both naked, and they felt no shame"?

4. What aspects of redemption are shared by men and women?

5. Study the passages of Scripture that deal with some of the women discussed in this chapter who were used by God in the Old Testament. What were some of their leadership characteristics? Which characteristics would you ask God to develop in you?

6. What lessons from the life of Jesus impressed you regarding women in the Gospels?

7. What encourages you from the examples of women in the early church?

8. Pray that God will give you the names of two or three other women who would meet with you to pray about developing a Women's Ministries Program in your church.

Two

CALLED
TO MINISTRY

Since Scripture confirms that Christian women in general are qualified for ministry, to what specific biblical ministry are women called? And what specific criteria further identify the woman called to that ministry?

Let's consider together a definitive passage, Titus 2:1–7, where Paul instructs the young pastor Titus in various aspects of his pastoral work.

> *You must teach what is in accord with sound doctrine. Teach the older men to be temperate, worthy of respect, self-controlled, and sound in faith, in love and in endurance.*
>
> *Likewise, teach the older women to be reverent in the way they live, not to be slanderers or addicted to much wine, but to teach what is good. Then they can train the younger women to love their husbands and children, to be self-controlled and pure, to be busy at home, to be kind, and to be subject to their husbands, so that no one will malign the word of God.*
>
> *Similarly, encourage the young men to be self-controlled. In everything set them an example by doing what is good.*

Paul the apostle was writing to a young pastor, Titus, whom he had left on the island of Crete. Paul evangelized and started small churches on Crete, and he left Titus with the responsibility to firmly establish those young churches so they would continue to expand and flourish.

However, there were serious problems in Crete, typical of any pagan society the gospel penetrates. First, they lacked role models to demonstrate what godly people were like. "In New Testament times, life in Crete had sunk to a deplorable moral level. The dishonesty, gluttony, and laziness of its people were proverbial."[1] No one was able to demonstrate what a godly husband and father looked like or to model how a Christian woman, wife, or mother should act.

Many young women coming to Christ today have not been reared in godly homes. Their parents may have been nominally Christian or attended church, but they did not demonstrate the reality of Christ in their daily routines. These young women truly don't know what a godly woman, wife, or mother looks like, and they desperately need that model. No one can model a godly Christian woman, except whom? A godly Christian woman!

The second problem we find in Titus 1:10. False teachers were deceiving and confusing people to the extent that Paul says in verse 16, "They claim to know God, but by their actions they deny him." We encounter this same problem today. More people now claim to be evangelical Christians in America than ever before, and yet we impact society even less. Christianity is losing its influence and its power because it has lost its distinctiveness. Sometimes it is difficult to discern the difference between believers and unbelievers. Therefore, as in the Crete of Paul's day, we have a need for proper role modeling.

As in Crete, we today have false teaching, and plenty of it. Without a biblical perspective, many women become confused, deceived, and dissatisfied. The biblical remedy of Titus 2 provides the antidote for false teaching and wrong behavior.

Sound teaching is the first element of that remedy. In Titus 2:1, Paul instructs Titus to "teach what is in accord with sound doctrine." In the Greek, the word *sound* means "healthy." In other words, the false teachings so rampant were sick and diseased. Paul starts with teaching. So often we attempt to change conduct without first appealing to the mind and will. But God begins with right teaching. Important as this is, however, right teaching reveals just one side of the coin.

Modeling correct behavior by godly people provides the second element of the remedy. Role models are needed that reflect the life of Jesus Christ. Christians must be distinguishable from unbelievers. Christian women must know what living out the life of Christ looks like in the flesh. God through Paul instructs Titus to teach the older men, the younger men, and the older women, as well, so as to set an excellent example for them. But when the Lord, through Paul, speaks of the teaching and training of the younger women, His instructions to Titus change. Titus is to prepare the older women to teach and model for the younger women a godly lifestyle.

Why Have a Woman-to-Woman Ministry?

In a day of increasing moral failure among the pastorate, the wisdom of woman-to-woman ministry is obvious. Surveys indicate that as many as 90 percent of moral failures in the pastorate begin in counseling women. Women, by contrast, have the freedom to follow up other women to encourage them in personal matters. If women are allowed to do the job God assigned to them, perhaps temptation toward immorality can be averted in the pastor's study.

However, numerous other reasons abound to demonstrate women's effectiveness in ministry to women. Who but another woman can fully understand all the differing aspects of pregnancy and childbearing, postpartum blues, and PMS? Women understand the cabin fever that often attacks in the preschool years that I call "a season of little feet." Another woman understands the mind weariness and isolation that can result from chasing energetic little ones who communicate primarily in one-syllable words and liberally spread sticky peanut butter and purple jelly on floors and walls.

Another woman can lift the spirits of a disappointed young wife who is discovering that her knight in shining armor leaves rust spots in the bathroom and socks on the floor. The older woman can help the young wife gain perspective, laugh at her circumstances, and dispel the fantasy that any knight comes rustproof in a fallen world. An older woman can encourage that younger woman to persist in love and hold on to her patience in her developing marriage. Another woman can share her own life experience as she learned how to balance the differing and demanding aspects of managing a home, loving a man, and rearing growing children.

A wise older woman becomes a resource in the case of sexual harassment or even abuse. She can be available to listen to, believe in, and intercede on behalf of a young woman trapped in a dangerous or abusive situation. She will be able to assist her in finding help and support from the leadership of the church or community.

A godly older woman points the younger woman to the only One who will never disappoint her and who is completely trustworthy in any and all of life's situations. She will instruct her from the Bible and from her own personal life about the journey of coming to know Him better.

What Are the Older Women to Model for the Younger Women?

Jesus pinpointed loving God and loving others as the core reality of life. Therefore, we can expect that the lives of the older women He desires to train younger women will reflect His priorities. Titus 2:1–7 (quoted earlier) describes the older woman God is calling to minister to younger women. It reveals the kind of woman God wants every younger woman to emulate. A study of the qualities demonstrated by these older women communicates the quality of their relationship with God and how they respond in significant relationships with others.

Reverent in the way they live, not to be slanderers or addicted to much wine, but to teach what is good. (Titus 2:3)

The first phrase, "reverent in the way they live," summarizes the kind of *positive relationship with God* the older woman demonstrates as well as how she will spend her time. The word translated "reverent" as used in the Greek language described a pagan priestess serving in the temple of her god. It carried the connotation of a full-time service of worship. Grasping that definition of *reverent* helps us to correct the misconception that life compartmentalizes into the sacred and secular. Rather, we understand that God desires women who view *all* of life as sacred and view themselves as serving God just as truly when they are preparing well-balanced, nutritious meals for an active family as when they are studying or teaching a Sunday school class. A woman such as this pursues a personal relationship with God with a deep passion. She values all of life equally, from the carpool to the corporation. She understands that God desires to be part of every activity, and that He needs women representing Him in every walk of life. Her personal commitment to Christ is an obvious qualification.

The second phrase, "not to be slanderers," reveals that *relationships should not be built on gossip and slander.* Relationships built on gossip become superficial relationships that counterfeit intimacy but do not lead to greater love of others or to a greater love and dependence upon God. Indeed, such relationships divert the heart from a passionate pursuit of God and divide individuals from one another. Paul warned of these superficial relationships when he spoke of the danger of young widows getting "into the habit of being idle and going about from house to house. And not only do they become idlers, but also gossips and busybodies, saying things they ought not to" (1 Timothy 5:13). That is why the ability to keep confidences is imperative if an older woman is to minister effectively to a younger woman.

As younger women share confidences, seeking God's perspective on the problems they have encountered, much information is communicated that would be very damaging if repeated and some of it may be shocking. It is important for the woman counseling a younger woman to be unshockable. The younger woman needs to feel loved and accepted as she communicates what is on her heart. That does not mean the one who listens must compromise and accept the young woman's sins. That is why this older woman needs a close relationship with God and a good knowledge of what God's Word teaches about moral living. But these younger women do need wise love and support if they are to choose to turn from sinful choices and move toward God.

This idea of trustworthiness is also a *protection for relationships.* The word *slanderer* is taken from the root word *diabolus,* or devil. Satan for centuries has used broken confidences, especially among women, to divide believers. A woman rooted personally in a deep relationship with God will not have the overwhelming need to pass on juicy tidbits simply to enhance her own popularity, and consequently her personal relationships will be protected.

The third descriptive phrase, "or addicted to much wine," adds another insight about this godly older woman. The specific Greek terms mean to be a drunkard. This phrase indicates how *not* to cope with life and the challenges of daily living. *God does not want us to avoid life and relationships by escaping from them through drink.* Escaping reality deadens the heart rather than developing character. I think that we could broaden the concept of addictive behaviors to include any kind of chemical dependence as well as other escape behaviors, such as soap operas, shopping, or extreme busyness. If we have not learned how to face life, depending on the Lord and His strength, rather than running from it, we will have little constructive counsel to share with another woman.

A young friend of mine was addicted to romance novels. She loved to read and spent hours each week reading fictional accounts of beautiful, romantic love affairs in which the fictional heroine was rescued from mundane routine by the handsome and often wealthy hero who carried her off to "happily ever after." Susan began to notice that she was tempted to compare her faithful and hardworking (if somewhat unromantic) husband most unfavorably to these fictitious heroes. After discussing this growing addiction and praying with an older woman, she chose to put aside a seemingly harmless pastime and instead invest that time in the study of the Scriptures. Her reading turned to biographies of men and women of God through the centuries. Her marriage improved.

If women ought not settle for superficial relationships or avoid relationships through escape or addiction, what positive instruction can we glean from the Scriptures? I believe that instruction comes in the phrase "teach what is good." This command suggests that, in addition to a passionate pursuit of God, an older woman will *invest her life in quality relationships,* especially with younger women, transmitting to the next generation the valuable lessons she has learned from God. By the time a woman begins to reach midlife, her own family responsibilities are changing. Her children may be away at school or married. She enjoys more time to invest in the lives of younger women. Interestingly, younger women will often listen to an older woman in this relationship even when they would not listen to their own mothers. In a similar way, midlife women find younger women eager to learn from them, even when their own daughters might not.

The word translated "good" means morally good, noble, or attractive. That assumes that the teacher understands what is good. I believe that understanding what is good requires a working knowledge of God's Word. It is important not only to know what the Bible says specifically but also to understand what it says in principle. Many of life's problems are not addressed verbatim in the Bible, but clear biblical principles can be found that speak to current decisions. The older woman who has grown to know God and the Bible can share those principles with a younger woman as no one else can.

What Good Things Do We Teach?

The subject matter to be taught by the older women to the younger women is described in Titus 2:4–5:

Then they can train the younger women to love their husbands and children, to be self-controlled and pure, to be busy at home, to be kind, and to be subject to their husbands, so that no one will malign the word of God.

INTEGRITY AND REALITY

In the *Amplified* translation of Titus 2:4–5, the Greek word translated "self-controlled" in the *New International Version* is further developed to read "sane and sober-minded—temperate and disciplined," which captures added aspects of training for younger women. Our counsel to them should promote integrity and reality. Those qualities make a significant difference in how a person lives. Escaping reality does not promote biblical living. Calling a younger woman back to "sanity" may involve recounting our own youthful "insanity" and how God brought us through similar experiences. That will require the willingness to be open and vulnerable. Although we should be able to share selectively and discreetly, the women we are counseling need to understand that their struggles are not unique to their marriage and children.

I recall a young woman who came to see me after only six months of marriage. Tearfully she spilled out her disillusionment with her husband and her fear that she had made a terrible mistake by marrying him. She wondered if it was too late to consider annulment. After listening briefly to the specific incidents she mentioned, I smiled gently and told her that what she was experiencing was common to almost every married couple in the process of learning to live together. My counsel to her was to go home, keep communicating, loving, adjusting, and forgiving—and to trust me that these adjustments could be made and that the Lord would supply her needs. I prayed with her and gave her a hug. About a year later she came to me all smiles and shared how much "things" had improved and thanked me for sending her back to the Lord and to her husband to persevere in the process of learning to share and give.

In the area of discipline and self-control, it is important that we understand that exhibiting those qualities does not just mean abstaining from impulses. (The inability to delay gratification is indicative of immaturity, whereas a growing ability to postpone gratification is an indication of growing maturity.) It also means learning to yield control to the Holy Spirit. Doing that will involve not only study of biblical teaching but also modeling the importance of depending upon God in daily situations and choosing to yield to His control.

Praying together effectively models how to turn a problem over to God. Many times I stirred supper on the stove with one hand while holding the phone in the other and saying, "Let's pray right now and ask God for His wisdom." Over and over I hear how God answered our prayers and how much the young wives were encouraged by our conversation and prayer. These times of prayer and conversation didn't prevent me from completing my responsibilities, and they accomplished something additional of eternal value. They also demonstrated how God is available anytime and my own dependence upon His wisdom. This willingness to talk or to give a word of counsel can turn a young woman toward God and transform her whole attitude.

In addition to promoting integrity and reality, our teaching of young women should *focus on her primary relationships.* For a married woman that would be her husband and children. For a single, younger woman that might be her parents and siblings or her roommate or business associates.

LOVE FOR HER HUSBAND

Scripture clearly instructs us to teach the younger women to love their husbands. The word used here is the Greek word *phileo. Phileo* is the love of human emotion, friendship, and enjoyment. I think young women, especially newlyweds, need older women to teach them to be adaptable and patient, to enjoy their mates without demanding perfection. Many of us learned this the hard way, but everyone doesn't have to learn everything by experience. I am amazed at how helpful it is to simply explain to a young woman the basic differences between men and women. When they say, "He won't do this, and he won't do that," I say, "You know, that is very typical of most men."

They are often shocked. "It *is?* You mean it isn't just my husband not being interested in what I say?"

I recently had the opportunity of speaking with a couple married for several years. As we discussed their difficulties, it was apparent that a common difference in the communication styles of men and women was a large part of the problem. When Leah inquired about what happened during Matthew's day at the office, he often replied, "Nothing." Conversation ended. Leah felt shut out and unimportant. As I was able to explain to Matthew Leah's true interest in the minor details of his daily experience, he was more than willing to give her more than his usual bottom-line response, "Nothing." As we discussed the general tendency of men to condense and women to amplify, I saw understanding dawn and brighten their faces.

As we talked further, it became apparent that Leah often frustrated Matthew with her lengthy accounts of her day with the children. She committed to attempt to condense her stories and leave time for his. I encouraged her to develop friendships with other women, who would enjoy hearing all the details she so enjoyed sharing.

There are other differences in the masculine and feminine viewpoints. Larry Crabb states, "Men are designed to enter their worlds of people and responsibilities with the confident and unthreatened strength of an advocate. Women are designed to invite other people into a nonmanipulative attachment that encourages the enjoyment of intimate relationship."[2] Because our fallen natures hinder our being all we were designed to be, there will be differences. When those differences lead to conflict, a confidential talk with an older woman can allow feelings to be shared and attitudes to be adjusted.

LOVE FOR HER CHILDREN

We are instructed to teach our younger women to love their children. Our world is increasingly hostile to children. With the legalization of abortion, many never make it to birth. Those who survive may experience all kinds of abuse from neglect to molestation. In fact, this has been the experience of some of the young women we mentor. They don't know what a normal childhood is.

Children need our protection, provision, discipline, and spiritual instruction. These require our presence. The training of children can't be done by making appointments during office hours. We must encourage the mothers of young children to choose, whenever possible, to stay at home with their children during those early years when they are so dependent and need to see the love of their parents demonstrated in tangible ways they can understand. This doesn't mean that a wife can't contribute to the family income. Many of the new small businesses starting today are by women working from their homes. With the expanding technology available today, this is not only possible but also preferable in many instances.

I am aware, also, that today many single mothers must work to support their families, and that introduces different and difficult problems. But we can encourage those who must of necessity work outside the home to look for childcare in home settings where the child's experience parallels a family atmosphere as much possible in contrast to a structured day care center. The statistics emerging on the emotional effect on children whose primary care has been in day care centers is not encouraging. Young women need experienced mothers to give them perspective and guidance during these critical years. Here the church can also provide support and wisdom.

MANAGEMENT OF HER HOME

The area of home management is often neglected in church training because it is not considered to be spiritual but secular. However, such a compartmentalization of life is not biblical. All of life is sacred. Therefore, it is important for the church to see home management as an appropriate subject of training for the younger women.

Since God assigns home management as the woman's area of responsibility, this responsibility requires appropriate authority. First Timothy 5:14 teaches that women are to "manage their homes." The word *manage* translated literally is "house despot." This gives emphasis to the area of a woman's home responsibility and authority. Some, unfortunately, teach biblical submission in such a restrictive way that while the woman's responsibility remains, the needed authority to accomplish it is removed. Instead of being, as I believe the Scripture teaches, the queen of her home, a wife often feels that she is simply a hired servant. Perhaps it is in rejecting this inaccurate and undervalued role that many middle class women have abandoned the arena of the home, leaving it increasingly cold and empty, while they seek self-fulfillment elsewhere. There is no doubt that today the home and the family have been severely damaged. Conversely, a home well managed by a loving woman given the appropriate authority and responsibility provides her with the legitimate satisfaction of a significant job well done.

However, we must remember that neither marriage nor motherhood nor career is intended to provide our deepest fulfillment or worth. Only Jesus Christ can do that. This important truth must also be taught to younger women as well.

Many basic homemaking skills are necessary if we are to obey God's directions about home management—and they are greatly needed by young wives today. Too many have come from homes where mothers didn't teach or model how to manage a home, or where mothers lacked the appropriate authority to manage with godly creativity. So there is a great need for the skills which many older women exercise almost automatically—skills in meal planning, cooking, baking, sewing, housekeeping, and time management. Her experience in those skills make the older women a valuable resource to young women today.

The high percentage of women working outside the home in this new millennium creates added pressure. Here it is important that husbands and wives share home duties, but the wife still needs to take the primary initiative in seeing that the home is well managed. Counsel with an older, godly woman can help a younger woman balance these demands of twenty-first century living.

Does this aspect of home management relate to loving your husband? I believe it does. When a man returns home from a difficult day in the office (wrestling in figurative terms with the thorns and thistles of the curse of Genesis 3:17–19) and comes into a home that is orderly and welcoming, he will be deeply encouraged that his efforts are accomplishing something, somewhere. His home, at least, reflects some sense of order in a world of chaos. Here, in the orderly home, we, as wives, reflect to him God's original design of a loving environment. Here, when a wife responds with care and attention to her home and learns to adapt herself to her husband, she ministers to his deepest longings for respect and a sense of adequacy.

"Men are different from women. They feel meaningfully encouraged not by a strong advocate who moves toward them but rather by a woman who appreciatively and respectfully accepts their efforts to handle the responsibilities of life."[3]

A wife who chooses that supportive role in the marriage, adapting herself to her husband, cooperates with God in demonstrating to her husband his unique value without in any way diminishing her own value and worth. Likewise, the wife who neglects the home and refuses to adapt to her husband communicates a lack of appreciation for his contribution to the home and a lack of a respect for his worth and value. With home management viewed as a significant ministry to one's husband, the most mundane of tasks take on eternal worth. Could it be possible that there might even be crowns for clean bathrooms, balanced meals, and all that laundry? I think so.

SUBMISSION TO HER OWN HUSBAND

Likewise, when a wife chooses to submit to her own husband, as to the Lord, she reinforces his value and worth as seen by God. She fuels his sense of adequacy for the task he is undertaking, even though he may be meeting resistance on the outside.

Unfortunately, the subject of submission has frequently suffered distortion in the way it has been taught. Such unbalanced teaching often causes women to grit their teeth at the mere mention of the word. Many women resent it, and more than a few men exploit it. However, it is important for men and women to understand that this is voluntary submission to a husband's leadership. It comes from a spirit of obedience to Jesus Christ. It is not something the husband is given permission to force upon an unwilling wife.

The word used for the obedience commanded of children and slaves is a different word from the word *submit*. Submitting is our responsibility before the Lord. It does not mean that all women are to submit to all men. It emphatically does not imply that women are inferior as persons to men. Man and woman were created equal in person in the sight of God to reflect His image (Genesis 1:27). A helpful parallel to consider is the Lord Jesus Christ, who chose to submit Himself in His humanity to the Father.

His submission in function in no way diminished His deity. Neither does a wife who submits to her own husband diminish her personhood in any way. Rather, she demonstrates her commitment to and trust in a sovereign God and ministers to her husband through the respect she gives him evidenced by her submission.

Ephesians 5 instructs the husband to lovingly and sacrificially lead his wife, and the wife to voluntarily submit to her husband's leadership. But neither can do those tasks without the control of the Holy Spirit. I like to picture biblical headship and submission not as a prison where a wife is restricted and oppressed but as a greenhouse where, under her husband's protection, provision, and with his blessing, she is encouraged to develop her full potential.

KINDHEARTEDNESS, A GOOD NATURE

This kindness is not simply smiling sweetly and saying nice things. It means *being* a good person and *doing* good deeds. First Timothy 5:9–10 says, "No widow may be

---

VICKIE'S PERSONAL TESTIMONY

We often don't realize God's blessing found in biblical submission. I learned this by hard experience. When I was married forty-nine years ago, there was no premarital counseling, nor were there the numerous books and courses on Christian marriage available today. My father died when I was seven, so I was not accustomed to male authority.

When Fred and I married, I really didn't think much about this submission stuff. It took nine years of stubbornness on my part and determination on my husband's part before the Lord penetrated my self-will with His Word. My husband and I were at an impasse. I wanted to do something he refused to have done. I was reading Ephesians 5 one day, and the Lord clearly spoke to me from the written page: "Wives submit to your husbands as to the Lord. For the husband is the head of the wife . . ."

But Lord, what if I'm right and he's wrong? What will happen if we don't do something about this problem right away? My imagination projected all kinds of terrible consequences if we didn't do things my way. But the Lord kept up the pressure, and finally I said, "Lord, I am Your child, and this is Your Word which I must obey. I want your will for my life more than I want my own way. I am willing for my husband to be an instrument in Your hands to show me your will. And I will trust You to give him the right decisions."

From then on, before I suggested a course of action to my husband, I would tell the Lord, "It's Your will I want. My husband's decision will be Your will for this situation."

It began to amaze me how many times we were in agreement. The tension and conflict caused by my insistence on my own way disappeared as I trusted God to speak to me through my husband.

This approach will serve a woman well, whether she is married to an unbeliever, an immature believer, or a strong leader. When we depend on God, making Him our refuge, to use the instruments He has provided for our guidance, He has a way of changing minds, wills, and actions to bring about His purposes.

---

put on the [official] list of widows unless she is over sixty, has been faithful to her husband, and is well known for her good deeds." Listen to how the Scripture describes her good deeds, such as "bringing up children." Did you realize that bringing up children is a called a good deed?

Often a young mother thinks, *I can't do anything for other people because I have so many things to do here at home.* God considers bringing up children a good deed as well as "showing hospitality, washing the feet of the saints, helping those in trouble and devoting [oneself] to all kinds of good deeds" (v. 10). That's kindness.

How do we teach kindness? By doing it. As we older women model it, the young women catch it. Galatians 6:10 teaches that we are to do good to everyone, especially to the family of God. This kindness starts with our families and with other believers and then reaches out beyond them to the hurting world around us.

Considering the quality of life within our own families, Tim Hansel often asks the women in his audience a searching question: "Are you fun to live with?" A willingness to forgive and to adapt and to cultivate a sense of humor adds zest to any marriage. I have a friend who loves to clip out cartoons and humorous articles and put them on her husband's plate for a smile at the end of a difficult day. A loving e-mail sent with an encouraging word can lighten a long and difficult workday. A welcoming smile goes a long way toward easing weariness and knitting relationships.

PURITY

This characteristic is very significant as related to loving your husband. Teaching purity would include teaching sexual chastity before marriage and fidelity in marriage. This unchanging biblical truth is desperately needed to counteract our present declining culture where sex has been so distorted and defiled that many people are genuinely surprised at what the Bible has to say about it. Popular sitcoms are based on ignoring the call for sexual purity. The accepted cultural views disregard this as irrelevant. It is not. Because Christians value purity, many people outside the church believe Christians are prudish and against the enjoyment of physical intimacy. Nothing could be further from the truth. Every biblical prohibition against sex relates to sex outside the marriage relationship. Within marriage, the sexual relationship is to be fully enjoyed and celebrated. Indeed, an entire book of the Bible, the Song of Solomon, describes in vivid detail the joys of the marriage relationship. It was designed by God to be enjoyed within marriage.

However, God had a design in mind for the sexual relationship. He designed marriage as a commitment without alternatives. Especially today when our culture affirms and promotes premarital sexual relations, where popular media characters model sexual involvement as routine, where violation of the marriage covenant and extramarital affairs are commonplace, and divorce continues to grow, we must address this issue head-on.

Especially today we must give clear, biblical instruction. First Corinthians 7:1–5 teaches both the *exclusivity* of the sexual relationship in marriage and the *gift* of the sexual relationship to be enjoyed within marriage. Additionally, we must teach that choosing sex outside of marriage may damage or preclude a meaningful and satisfying relationship in marriage. Sex is not simply a "right" to be enjoyed in whatever way is satisfying for the moment, but this God-given gift is a treasure to be guarded and celebrated within biblical guidelines.

Someone told me recently that her husband deserted her and their four children because he was in love with another woman. He admitted that he knew what he had done was wrong but said that after the divorce and remarriage he would ask forgiveness of God and be restored. Did he think he was fooling God? However, I am afraid that his thinking represents a more prevalent view than we would like to admit, even within the evangelical church.

Sex within marriage is an important part of the ongoing relationship between husband and wife. Women need other women to encourage them to understand both the privilege and the responsibility of the sexual relationship. A neglect of the physical aspects of marriage can put the relationship at risk. The Bible is clear that the physical relationship is to continue regularly except for a season of prayer for particular reasons. The decision for abstinence must be by mutual consent and for a brief time (1 Corinthians 7:1–5). (And, of course, there are times when for reasons of health there must be restraint.)

A woman committed to purity and faithfulness in this sexual area honors the Lord and is a blessing to her family.

LIVING SO THAT THE WORD OF GOD WILL NOT BE DISCREDITED

Should one need further motivation to support woman-to-woman ministry, Titus 2:5 concludes by emphasizing that women who follow the examples of godly older women provide no occasion for the Word of God to be discredited.

That statement underscores the fact that the world observes the lives of those who claim to belong to God. When our lives look no different from the prevailing culture regarding home and family, and when our character does not reflect purity and kindness—in other words, when we do not love our husbands and children in demonstrable ways—the world will discount the truth and validity of the Word of God.

A friend of Gwynne's, John, took the Dale Carnegie course "How to Win Friends and Influence People." At the conclusion of the course the instructor challenged the class: "Men and women, I hope that you will use all we have studied and that your lives will reflect these principles. I can't imagine a more disappointing experience than for you to tell someone you have taken the Dale Carnegie course and for them to reply, '*You? You* have taken the Dale Carnegie course? I *never* would have guessed.'"

Several years later John encountered a mutual friend acquainted with his instructor. In conversation John shared that their mutual friend had been his Dale Carnegie instructor. To which, to John's amusement and amazement, the man replied, "He, he *taught* the Dale Carnegie course? I can't believe it! He is one of the most reclusive and unfriendly people I know!"

I have often reflected on this story as it illustrates what we *say* when we are talking about our Christian walk versus how we actually *live* our Christian lives. When the two don't match up, at least in measure, all validity is lost. Conversely, when our lives reflect the truth of God, others will be drawn to God and they will seek to know what makes us different.

Jesus instructed us, "Let your light shine before men, that they may see your good deeds and praise your Father in heaven" (Matthew 5:16). A woman's life well lived in dependence upon God in purity and kindness is one of the most effective tools for evangelism.

An effective Women's Ministry Program can greatly enhance the development of this kind of attractive lifestyle for women. And, in turn, when a church recognizes its responsibility to provide this ministry for its women, the entire church will benefit. When women are available to each other, the words of Psalm 92:14, which state, "They will still bear fruit in old age," will be fulfilled. We must never retire from fruit bearing. As the family of God begins to compensate for the breakup of the extended family, we can provide a support system for the generations that will follow us.

In my own life, when I was twenty-eight years old, married with one little boy, and defeated at my lack of consistency in my faith, I was truly at the end of my rope. I told the Lord that if He could not make me a stable, consistent Christian I simply did not want to live any longer. I was attending a women's Bible study taught with compassion and love by a single woman fifteen years my senior. She took an interest in me and asked me to teach a small study, especially to benefit a woman recently converted from a cult. For five years I taught that small class, never more than a dozen women, in her home and in her presence. She helped me discover my gifts and develop them. She encouraged me, corrected me, and loved me.

As a result of her influence and training, other opportunities opened to me. Thirty-four years ago my husband and I left our home to study for full-time ministry. This woman had more influence on my life than any other person outside my family. Any benefit derived from my teaching today must also be credited to the account of this older single woman who invested her life in me.

Questions for Study and Discussion

1. Read Titus 2:1–5. Why do you think Paul instructed Titus to train the older women but not the younger women?

2. Describe an older woman of your acquaintance who you think demonstrates a reverent lifestyle.

3. Why do you think slander and gossip might lead to superficial and destructive relationships? What activities might contribute to slander and gossip?

4. What addictive behaviors can be used as an escape from involvement for Christ in the lives of other women?

5. Discuss the concept of reality and integrity as related to the command in Titus 2:4–5 (AMP) to train the younger women to be sane and sober-minded.

6. Read Titus 1:8; 2:14; 3:1, 8. What new insights regarding good works did you learn? How might you apply this to a woman's life?

7. What do you think 1 Timothy 5:14 teaches about a woman's responsibility for her home? What are the practical outworkings of this responsibility regarding the handling of finances, the checkbook, time management, meal preparation, and home decorating, to name but a few?

8. Which aspect of learning to love your husband was a new thought to you from this chapter?

9. How important do you think it is for the sexual relationship to be taught in a positive manner? What older woman in your church might you ask to teach on this subject?

Note

1. *NIV Study Bible* (Grand Rapids: Zondervan, 1973), Introduction to Titus; notes at 1:2; 1:12.
2. Larry Crabb, *Men and Women* (Grand Rapids: Zondervan, 1991), 212.
3. Ibid., 167.

Part Two

CONSIDERING THE FIELD

You are God's field.
1 CORINTHIANS 3:9

Three

IDENTIFYING
THE NEEDS

Several years ago the Women's Ministries Program of Northwest Bible Church in Dallas, Texas, arrived at the place where you may be today. The newly elected Women's Ministries Board decided to take a hard look at the programs in place for many years. Much effective ministry had been accomplished through those programs, but the percentage of women participating from the entire church body was small, and many women, especially the younger women, were not involved at all. That prevented the intergenerational dynamic at the heart of God's plan for a Women's Ministries program from occurring.

This intergenerational need had become clear to me several years previously. I had been teaching women in retreats and Bible studies for a number of years. I was also teaching a weekly Bible study for women in a local church that had an outreach to women all over the area. The younger women repeatedly said how much they appreciated learning the Bible from an older woman who had been where they were. They appreciated relevant application of the Scripture to their specific concerns.

My husband and I saw this as a specialized area of ministry and founded Titus 2:4 Ministries, Inc., in 1984, really to define what I was already doing. As I traveled to speak throughout the United States, however, I encountered this same need among women everywhere. Then, when my husband and I traveled to Manila and participated in Lausanne II, we discovered this need for women to minister to women, for each generation to nurture and disciple the next, was expressed by women all around the world. This conviction continues to be confirmed as I have spoken to women in Latin

America, Eastern Europe, the Middle East, and Canada. Women around the world, in very different cultures, share more in common as women than they experience differences due to culture.

At Northwest Bible Church the existing women's program was built around circles for Bible study, meeting monthly in homes. Although they enjoyed the advantage of closer fellowship in these small groups, something seemed to be missing, and general interest was declining. After considerable prayer, the new board made the decision to suspend all activities for one year and invest that year in research and prayer. They began by developing the survey that appears later in this chapter ("Improved Women's Ministries Survey") and distributing it to all the women of the church in order to determine their interests and needs.

In addition to surveying the women of the church, the women on the board also contacted churches around the country where successful Women's Ministries flourished. They were looking for the qualities these programs shared in common that made them effective. The committee discovered several common features:

- Women wanted more sessions, not less—weekly, rather than monthly
- Bible study, not projects or missions, should be the main focus
- Diversity was essential, for example, electives based on interests
- Programs with a woman on the church staff had greater continuity and effectiveness

As we further developed and refined these common features, we identified twelve elements of an effective women's ministry. They are as listed below and will be discussed in the next chapter.

An Effective Women's Ministries Program

- Starts with prayer
- Knows its people
- Enlists church leadership
- Articulates specific goals
- Is led by women
- Identifies and develops leadership
- Is founded on Bible study
- Develops variety
- Provides support groups
- Encourages outreach
- Encourages personal friendships
- Remains flexible and relevant

IMPROVED WOMEN'S MINISTRIES SURVEY
*(Please participate in our survey and assist us in designing a women's ministry
that will meet your needs and give you opportunities to exercise your gifts.)*

There are different kinds of gifts, but the same Spirit. There are different kinds of service, but the same Lord. . . . to each one now the manifestation of the Spirit is given for the common good (1 Corinthians 12:4–5, 7).

What area of need would you like to see met by the Women's Ministries Program?

_____ Worship   _____ Instruction

_____ Community   _____ Evangelism

What are your areas of interest (check as many as you would like)?

_____ Community outreach	_____ Mothers' encouragement
_____ Hospital visitation	_____ Exercise
_____ Bible study	_____ Weight reduction support
_____ Discipleship	_____ International students
_____ Prayer	_____ Senior Adult Fellowship
_____ Lay counseling	_____ Hospitality for new members
_____ Political action groups	_____ Missions
_____ Food ministry	_____ Church grounds beautification
_____ Sewing	_____ Support groups
_____ New skills (homemaking)	_____ Other

RELEVANT PERSONAL DATA:

Age: _____

Children's Ages: _____

Marital and family status: _____
(Single, married, widowed, divorced, blended family)

Do you work outside the home? _____ Full Time: _____ Part Time: _____

Have you had other experience in Women's Ministries? _____

How far do you live from the church? _____
What time is more convenient for you? (Circle one)   Mornings   Evenings

Please use the space below and the reverse side for any comments, questions, or suggestions.

Questions for Study and Discussion

* * * * * * * * * * * *

1. How large is your church?

2. When was your church established?

3. What kinds of ministries to women have there been thus far?

    A. List the three most effective:

    (1)

    (2)

    (3)

        (a) What percentage of your women attend?

        (b) What are the ages of those involved?

    B. List the three least effective:

    (1)

    (2)

    (3)

        (a) What percentage of the women attend?

        (b) What are the ages of those involved?

4. What are the predominant ages in your congregation?

5. How would you describe your church—urban, rural, suburban? Other unique characteristics?

6. How do these characteristics affect your women or your planning for a Women's Ministries Program?

7. List some of the ideas that have come to mind as you have read this material and prayed.

8. List the ways that you can utilize technology to benefit your women's ministry (i.e., computers, e-mail, etc.). Developing a data base early can save a lot of time later on.

9. Does your church have a Web site? Can women's ministry be given a part of that site? Would you like to develop your own Web site? Do you have the personnel for this?

10. What five ways can you pray specifically for the development of your women's ministry?

F o u r

DEVELOPING A
BIBLICAL PHILOSOPHY

Toward the end of the last chapter we listed twelve elements of an effective Women's Ministries Program. In this chapter we want to examine each of those elements in some detail, because we believe a ministry to women without a core philosophy behind it will flounder and ultimately fail. Use these elements to develop a philosophy for your ministry; they will provide guidelines for setting your priorities and making decisions.

An Effective Women's Ministries Program
Starts with Prayer

Even if you are the only one interested in developing a Women's Ministries Program, begin to pray and ask God to give you one or two other women willing to meet with you and pray. Include the pastor's wife if at all possible. As you three or four meet regularly to pray, begin to ask God about some of the following issues:

1. How open is the leadership of the church to a Women's Ministries Program?
2. Do you presently have a program for women? How effective is it?
   a. Are you personally involved in the present ministry?
   b. How open to change are those involved to evaluation and expansion?
   c. Would potential leadership meet with you to pray and plan?
   d. When should you involve your pastor as you begin?

3. What kind of resource people do you have among your church women?
4. Whom could you enlist for leadership and support for the ministry?
5. How should you approach both church leadership and other women?
6. What direction should your ministry to women take?
7. How do you sense God might have you begin?
8. How can God use you to encourage and strengthen your church?
9. How can God use you to encourage and strengthen your pastor?
10. Ask God to protect you from a critical and impatient spirit; change comes slowly.

An Effective Women's Ministries Program Knows Its People

Using as an example the survey provided in the previous chapter, develop such a tool to gain a clearer understanding of your particular group of women. You will acquire important information for planning purposes: the needs and interests expressed, the experience in your group, how many women are working outside the home, the general age breakdown. From this information you can begin to evaluate various specific aspects of any proposed program. Should the group meet in the evening or in the daytime, or both? What has been the previous history of the Women's Ministries Program at your church, and how will that impact your planning? How far do your women travel to the church? Is yours an urban church or a neighborhood church? The answers to each of these questions will influence the various decisions you make as you develop your program.

The more of your women that you can survey, the more effectively you can plan and the more relevant your program can be. Be creative in reaching all the women of the congregation, whether or not they expressed interest previously. Often the survey can be included in the church bulletin, even over a period of several weeks. In addition, if your church has a Web site, the survey can be posted there, completed and returned by e-mail, or if your church sends e-mail notifications, perhaps they could send every woman the survey by e-mail as well.

An Effective Women's Ministries Program Enlists Church Leadership

A key step in organizing a Women's Ministries Program is to inform and educate the male leadership of the church, especially if they do not share your vision. Their support is crucial to the long-term success of women's ministry. It is a rare exception to find leadership that places a Women's Ministries Program high on its agenda. Usually the leadership leaves that to the women to do for themselves, including paying the expenses. We can respectfully point out that there is nothing in the Bible about a youth, college, or singles' ministry, but Titus 2:3–4 gives a definite command for the older women to teach and train the generation following them.

Although we take an offering at our Women's Ministries events, all our expenses, including childcare, are included in the overall church budget. This concept developed as we ministered over the years. We continue to run a tight ship and do all we can to "pay our own way," but we have the comfort of knowing that if we are not completely successful we have the support of the entire church. (The offering received is deposited in the church general fund.)

Some denominational churches have a women's organization already in place with a structure that has been the same for a hundred years: WMU, WOC, WMS. Often these programs in their original form do not adequately meet the needs of today's woman without significant revision. When a key older woman from one of these groups supports the new approach, the transition can be much less disruptive. Ask God to give you such a visionary older woman.

ORGANIZED AND THOUGHTFUL PLANNING

The women from Northwest Bible Church compiled a written proposal (see Appendix 1 for an outline of the material contained in that proposal). They included quotations from well-known women about the need for a relevant ministry to women and quotations from women in their own church in response to the survey. They detailed the plans they had in mind. They demonstrated their conviction that a woman was needed on staff to administer the program. Then they invited the elders and their wives for dinner and presented each elder with a folder containing the detailed program laid out clearly. They answered questions and discussed the subject thoroughly. This thorough approach and the evidence the women offered convinced the elders, and, consequently, a salary for a Minister to Women was included in the next year's budget, and I was hired. Expenses for a Women's Ministries Program were also budgeted—including childcare expenses. I can't emphasize enough how important it is to provide childcare at no cost to the mothers bringing their children. These women are the very ones we want to reach, and if we make the cost prohibitive we will defeat our own purposes.

A PROTECTED AND SUPPORTIVE ENVIRONMENT

I believe the elders of Northwest Bible Church demonstrated the kind of enlightened leadership essential for a vital Women's Ministries Program to thrive in a local church. It is imperative that the pastor and elders understand the need to provide for the women of the church. They should recognize that women have needs only women can meet. Paul's exhortation to Titus (Titus 2:3) should demonstrate that women have needs only women can meet. They must delegate that ministry to spiritually mature women who can design and implement the program. Church leadership for its part must provide the facilities, personnel, and money necessary as an integral part of the church program. Women should not have to run a bootleg program on the side supported only with bake sales and garage sales. I view the relationship of the Women's Ministries Program to the overall church ministry much as the relationship of a wife to her husband. The husband provides the environment for the wife to accomplish the ministry given to her by God in the home. That supportive environment includes providing the finances necessary to accomplish their mutual goals. In the same way, when a church invests its funds to equip women, the entire church will reap handsome returns.

An Effective Women's Ministries Program Articulates Specific Goals

The development of specific goals keeps a Women's Ministries Program continually on track and provides a measure of its direction and effectiveness. Some suggested goals are:

- To minister to the needs of our church women
- To encourage growth toward spiritual maturity
- To encourage outreach through missions and evangelism
- To equip women to serve others in the church
- To provide opportunities for ministry to the community

These are the kinds of long-range goals that must be kept in mind as the whole ministry is planned and implemented.

An Effective Women's Ministries Program Is Led by Women

STAFF POSITIONS

Of course, I am biased about the need for a woman on the church staff for women. Call her what you will—Minister to Women, Pastor to Women, Director of Women's Ministries, or Chairman of the Women's Ministries Board. You may have to start with a volunteer, but don't give up the idea that this position deserves a salary, whether the woman filling it is a part-time or full-time staff member.

A staff person can focus her attention full-time on the needs of women, both corporately and individually. She can plan and implement long-range programs that enjoy continuity. Because she meets regularly with the church staff she can speak for women, correlate the Women's Ministry with all other church activities, and add the relational insight that women bring to leadership. In most churches women make up more than half of the constituency, and they are usually unrepresented on the church staff. In a number of delicate counseling situations, I have been able to share with our pastoral staff the issue from a woman's perspective. They heartily thanked me for it. A staff member can be more regularly available for personal counseling, which can become an important aspect of the ministry. Her ability and availability to counsel women provide the protective aspect of the ministry mentioned earlier.

Here is an excerpt of a letter I received from a young woman that illustrates the importance of having the women's ministry directed by a staff woman:

Your stability in serving at Northwest to the women is an intangible ministry. Your commitment through the years is an unspoken anchor in this society of constant change. The fact that you've been there, involved in women's lives, is one of the threads that binds the newer folks to the ones who've been involved for years.

I remember being amazed at how open our discussion group was from the very beginning, and I think the fact that you had built into the lives of so many of those women for such a long time allowed them the freedom to open up.

At the present time women are graduating from seminaries and Bible colleges who have been highly trained and could fill these positions if churches realized the need for a staff person to oversee women's ministries.

The goal of the staff woman should be to equip others to do the job, not to do it all herself. She is a pacesetter, not a prima donna. Delegating to other women an opportunity to serve in a position for which she is gifted sets her up for success, and she will want to keep serving. This delegation requires honesty, humility, and discernment on the part of the leader.

WOMEN'S MINISTRY BOARD

In addition, and equally important, a Women's Ministries Board will be the heartbeat of an effective Women's Ministries Program. The size of the board will depend on the size of your church. The job descriptions for our board are found in chapter 7 as an example. We update them each year.

The present chairman and I select the new chairman. We choose her from current board members serving their second year. There is a new chairman each year. Each one I have served with led in a different style, but each was wonderfully efficient and indispensable to me. We consult frequently, and she takes care of communicating with the board and Women's Ministries about responsibilities, opportunities, and coming events; chairs the board meetings; and generally assists all the board members as they need it.

My job description is also included in chapter 7, because the chairman will have to assume many of those responsibilities if you do not have a woman on your church staff.

To get started, if your church does not have a staff person for women, the pastor can appoint a woman with spiritual maturity and organizational skills to serve as Chairman (or Director) of Women's Ministries. Then she should pray and seek other women to work with her as a team, women who have a love and vision for women. As your program develops, you will find various categories of activities demand supervision. That is why it is important to have a board of several members, each of whom has an area for which she is responsible. Authority goes with responsibility. The coordinator should be free to be creative and innovative within the guidelines set by the board. No member of the board can be a loose cannon doing her own thing. The board should discuss each area and cooperate with the person in charge of it. That will provide accountability, yet allow each woman to use the unique gifts God has given her. This freedom with supervision is the secret of achieving the variety that makes a program successful. The Chairman (or Director) cannot be a dictator, demanding everything be done her own way. That may be difficult for her if she is a strong leader. Yet it is especially important to be flexible if you want to attract younger women. They often will not fit into our old forms or traditional ways of doing things. Do not elevate forms or methods to the status of the inerrancy of Scripture. Never say, "We've never done it like that before!" or, "It won't work!" Be open to new ideas. Design the program to meet the needs of your women, and the women you would like to reach, rather than forcing the women into an outmoded form.

I learned a good lesson one year in planning for our Christmas luncheon. Susan, the board member responsible for special events, came up with the theme of a Mexican fiesta. I am not overly fond of that cuisine and wasn't particularly excited about the menu or all the details required to pull it off. However, remembering my commitment to allow flexibility and freedom within the leadership, I agreed with her plan, though without much enthusiasm. The end result was an outstanding luncheon, enjoyed by everyone and much appreciated. I could have squelched this delightful opportunity if I had demanded that every aspect of the program be as I would individually prefer it. I would have robbed Susan of the opportunity to minister to the entire body with her creative and artistic gifts. I was glad to admit I was wrong.

Our Women's Ministries Board meets monthly for business. We do not have any men at our meetings, either elders or staff. They have delegated the job to us. We are, however, accountable to the Elder Board and must follow their guidelines and report to them when requested, but they trust us to do the job. The Women's Ministries Board also meets for prayer just before the Women's Ministries Session on Tuesdays and every other week after the Women's Ministries Session. As a staff person, I report to the associate pastor on a regular basis. An organizational chart of our Women's Ministries Program is found in chapter 7.

EXPOSING THE MYTH

The myth that if you give women an inch they will take over the church is just that—a myth. If you give women significant ministry in the very area God has commanded for them, a ministry to the many, very real needs of women, they will be so busy and so fulfilled that the resentment and restlessness they often feel will find no fertile ground in which to flourish. Exposing this misconception about women will benefit your entire congregation.

An Effective Women's Ministries Program Identifies and Develops Leadership

The first consideration in developing leadership is an understanding of giftedness. It is important to match people to the tasks for which they are gifted. Because I believe that God provides gifted women to meet the needs of each congregation, it is helpful here to consider what the Bible teaches about spiritual gifts. Some women do not realize that they have been equipped from the time of salvation with special abilities from the Holy Spirit to strengthen their fellow believers (1 Corinthians 12:7).

Because an effective Women's Ministries Program requires a team effort, we help women identify their gifts. We must find out what individual women like to do and what they do well. We need also to observe when and where a woman's service is not effective. We in leadership should do that for ourselves as well. A wise leader recognizes that she doesn't do everything equally well. Where I am weak, someone else is strong, and if we are working together, her strength supports my weakness.

> A SPIRITUAL GIFT IS A SUPERNATURAL CAPACITY
> FREELY AND GRACIOUSLY GIVEN BY
> THE SOVEREIGN GOD AT THE TIME OF A PERSON'S
> SALVATION, ENABLING THAT PERSON
> TO MINISTER TO OTHERS FOR THE PURPOSE
> OF ACCOMPLISHING GOD'S WORK.

There are several reasons you and your women should understand and exercise spiritual gifts. When we in leadership are careful to fit women into jobs that suit their gifts, they will enjoy doing them, do them successfully, and be willing to take on new responsibilities as their confidence increases. Conversely, when you place a woman in an area where she is not gifted, she often finds the job so burdensome and unrewarding that she is reluctant to serve again.

KNOWING YOUR GIFTS GIVES YOU AN INDICATION OF GOD'S WILL

When people know how God has gifted them for service, it will be helpful to them to determine where God wants them to serve. Many times a person has more than one gift, so do not limit service to just the most obvious or the one most often used.

KNOWING YOUR GIFTS HELPS YOU SET PRIORITIES

If you understand your gifts, it will help you resist saying yes to every opportunity that comes to you. You can choose to serve in areas fitted to the gifts God has given you, and you won't feel that nagging guilt for saying no to other opportunities. In fact, as you recognize the way the gifts benefit the body of Christ, you will see that to accept something God hasn't called you to do will rob someone else in the body of the opportunity to exercise her gifts.

KNOWING YOUR GIFTS HELPS YOU ACCEPT YOURSELF

Often when considering service we make the mistake of comparing ourselves to others with different gifts, particularly the public gifts, and begin to feel inadequate. When a woman discovers her own gifts and begins to serve in those capacities, she experiences the satisfaction of serving as God designed her. That experience develops in her a growing sense of satisfaction and fulfillment and self-acceptance.

KNOWING YOUR GIFTS IDENTIFIES AREAS NEEDING DEVELOPMENT

Additionally, when a woman discovers her spiritual gifts, she then has direction for prayer and development.

For instance, if you have the gift of teaching, perhaps you would like to pursue further education or take seminars to develop your speaking and teaching skills. Perhaps you have the gift of exhortation or mercy. Maybe counseling training would sharpen and develop those gifts. If your gift happens to be the gift of giving, perhaps you would find a key place in the missions program of your church, studying the various agencies requesting support.

GIFTS MENTIONED IN THE NEW TESTAMENT

1 Corinthians 12

Message of wisdom	Message of knowledge
Faith	Gifts of healing
Miraculous power	Prophecy
Distinguishing between spirits	Speaking unlearned languages
Apostles	Teaching
Helpers	Administration

Romans 12:1–8
Serving
Encouraging
Contributing to needs
Exercising leadership
Showing mercy

Ephesians 4
Evangelist
Pastor/teacher

The important thing to remember is that spiritual gifts are given not simply for our own benefit but for the building up of others in the body of Christ. Therefore, we really don't have an option about using them. When a member of your physical body stops functioning, the whole body is sick. The same holds true when a member of Christ's body does not use her gifts for the good of the rest of the members. The whole local body suffers loss. Romans 12:5 tells us that we belong to one another. We are not our own to live life totally independent of one another, focused on pleasing ourselves.

I delight to make women feel special, as they are, but we must also challenge each one that she is uniquely gifted by God with influence in her sphere of relationships.

We must remind each woman that God holds her responsible to use her influence to serve Christ by ministering to others. Ministry that only pampers or entertains does not draw a woman toward her full potential and on to spiritual maturity.

HOW TO DISCERN YOUR SPIRITUAL GIFT

1. Start with prayer, individually and with others. Ask God to reveal your gift.
2. Study what the Bible has to say about spiritual gifts.
3. Ask God's people what they observe about your abilities and effectiveness.
4. Examine your strongest desires or interests.
5. Look for an opportunity to serve in that capacity.
6. Allow God to confirm by experience and the feedback of others.
7. Notice the area in which you experience joy and ease in exercising your gift with results beyond expectations.

Additionally, there are many spiritual gift tests that help confirm or inform people about their gifts. One test is published by Church Growth Institute, P. O. Box 4404, Lynchburg, VA 24502-0404. Another is the *Trenton Spiritual Gifts Analysis* published by the Charles E. Fuller Institute of Evangelism and Church Growth, P. O. Box 91990, Pasadena, California 91109-1990. We offered these tests to our women when I taught a series on 1 Corinthians 12. Many women said that they were surprised at what the tests indicated, but as a result they could see possibilities they had not previously considered. However, the tests should be confirmation of the other factors just listed.

An Effective Women's Ministries Program Is Founded on Bible Study

Bible study should be the central focus of a vital Women's Ministries Program. God's Word is what people hunger and thirst for, often without realizing that the Bible is what they need. You can draw women to varied programs that interest them, but you will not have the steady spiritual growth you desire without consistent teaching of the Scriptures as relevant to the lives of women today. The goal of an effective ministry should always be to develop spiritual maturity (Ephesians 4:11–13; 1 Peter 2:2).

A church Women's Ministries Program cannot enforce the stringent rules of some parachurch organizations. Those rules suit their particular purpose and structure, but a church program must be designed to meet the needs of all the women of the church. These women are found at many different spiritual levels—young lambs and mature sheep. Since the Women's Ministries Programs provide opportunity for women to invite their neighbors and friends to a church-sponsored event, your audience will range from believers and new believers, the scripturally untaught, to the spiritually mature and knowledgeable in the Scriptures.

That is why your Bible teaching must include the gospel frequently for those who have not yet come to faith; be clear for the new learner, yet also challenge the mature Christian. That is not an easy assignment, but it is possible.

WHAT AND HOW LONG TO STUDY

Today's culture is not geared to lengthy commitments. Sometimes it is advantageous to divide the study year into three sessions of between six and ten weeks each. Fall sessions can begin in mid-September and end in mid-November. That frees the women for the holiday season. The winter session begins the week after New Year's week and ends in mid-March. We take one week off during school spring break and hold the spring session from late March through mid-May. This approach makes it possible to study different subjects each session. Others find two sessions, fall and spring, beneficial.

There are many advantages to these shorter, complete sessions. For one thing, it is much easier to get a teacher for six, seven, eight, or nine weeks than to find someone willing to teach from September to May. That is true of securing elective leaders as well. I am often asked what material we use for Bible study. Our teachers have always prepared their own studies, but that is not a requirement. We have had studies of Bible books, character studies, and topical studies.

Some of the Bible series I have taught over the past several years are available on audiotape. Those are listed in Appendix 2. They can be ordered if they would be helpful to your group. Individual questions that allow a person to study the passage before she comes to class will challenge the serious student and help the new one learn to use the Bible in personal study. Everyone won't answer the questions, but those who do say without exception that they benefit from them. Examples of questions for this home study are also in Appendix 2.

In addition, many excellent study books for women by women are available in bookstores. Some authors I might suggest would be Jill Briscoe, Dee Brestin, Cynthia Heald, Carol Kent, and the authors of the various studies in the Women's Workshop Series. There are also new videotaped series available as well.

WHO WILL TEACH?

Who will teach? This is where much dependence on the Lord is necessary. First, the teacher should be a woman. I have surprised men when I have been invited to speak to them in seminary classes, and I've stated, "Women can teach and apply the Scriptures to women better than men can." When I humorously observe that most of their illustrations come from football, baseball, or the military, they usually get my point. A woman teacher has an empathy and understanding that communicates to women. Women respond more openly to a woman and come more readily for personal counsel, which is a vital aspect of the ministry.

But suppose you believe you don't have a woman in your church who can teach. Does that mean you must go outside your church for leaders? Not necessarily. I am persuaded that God gives each local body the spiritually gifted people necessary to bring that particular body to maturity, including spiritually gifted women, so I believe there probably is a woman in the church who can fill this role. Pray for guidance. I cannot overemphasize the importance of praying about every aspect of your program. Also, be very careful that you look for a person who teaches the *Bible.* It is easy to be captivated by a good storyteller or someone with a charismatic personality who just talks about emotions and experiences, or who keeps you laughing. She might throw in a Bible verse here or there, but that is not systematic Bible teaching, and you will not have steady spiritual growth from that type of message.

Is there a woman in your church who teaches a home Bible study? Is there a woman who has been involved in parachurch Bible studies, such as Bible Study Fellowship or Community Bible Studies? Is there a person who always blesses you when she teaches? Is there a woman most people consider to be a godly example and knowledgeable in the Scriptures? Ask her if she would be willing to teach one lesson or a four- or six-week session in the Women's Ministries Program. Start small. Maybe she has prepared a series for use elsewhere. You can evaluate her effectiveness in speaking to a large group. Some people are very effective in small groups, but not as much so in larger groups. We try to look for women who project a personal warmth and love for women—a woman with compassion and humor. The teacher functions as an important role model while she teaches.

If you find you truly do not have anyone in your church who can take on the task, you could begin by asking a good teacher in the community to start you off, but try not to depend on importing people. One of your primary goals is to develop the gifts of your own women, and that will never happen if they keep seeing "experts" do the job.

One church in our area asked me to start their Bible study series. I told them that I would come and teach a seven-week series at the end of their Women's Ministries year if they used their own women before that. They didn't think anyone would do it, but they found three women willing to take four weeks each. I came in at the end of that year and taught the seven-week series, but they have never needed me again because they had found several in their own body willing to develop their gift of teaching. Keep praying and expecting! Even though it can be easier to use an excellent video, or to import an expert, ask God to enable you to develop women in your own body. This will personalize, deepen, and strengthen your ministry to your own women as well as develop the women God has given your congregation.

An Effective Women's Ministries Program Develops Variety

VARIETY IN THE WEEKLY PROGRAM

We have found that dividing our weekly program into two segments meets a variety of needs. In the first part of the program we gather for Bible study together. Then we allot fifteen minutes for announcements, service opportunities, testimonies, special music, and an offering. During the second half of the program we offer various electives or interest groups. These range from developing spiritual and practical skills to support groups. An extensive list of electives we have offered in the small groups appears in chapter 8.

BENEFITS OF ELECTIVES

- Women have an opportunity to serve the Lord using all their skills. They are not limited only to Bible teaching or working in the kitchen or nursery. If, as Scripture teaches, all of life is ministry, then our professional women—the lawyer, financial planner, nurse, and counselor—can profitably share their knowledge with us and increase their impact and ministry. The homemaker can teach basic skills, such as cooking, sewing, time management, and hospitality. The mature mothers can teach child rearing from babies to adult children. All of life's training and experience become resources for the electives. This greatly expands opportunity for ministry and leadership development.
- Women to get to know each other because the group is smaller and they meet for several weeks. Many friendships begin here and continue.
- Women learn some skill (spiritual or practical) that they have needed or wanted to learn. So they grow in ability and confidence.
- Women learn to care and pray for each other because we allot fifteen minutes of the elective time for sharing and prayer. Many women pray aloud for the first time in this small group, because it's safe.

• Women's gifts are discovered. The electives provide an obvious way to spot new leaders for Women's Ministries. Most of the women on our board have helped teach an elective. Many continue to do so after their term on the board is complete.

PROGRAM SCHEDULE

9:30–9:40	Group singing
9:40–10:15	Bible lesson
10:15–10:30	Announcements, recruiting, offering, special music
10:30–11:45	Elective time
	(including 15 minutes of prayer and sharing)

We hold a training session for the small group leaders before the fall session of the Women's Ministries Program to go over the elective leaders' guidelines and to provide some training on how to lead a small group. A resource book we suggest is *How to Lead Small Groups,* by Neal F. McBride (Colorado Springs: NavPress, 1990). We tape the orientation session so new leaders coming in during the year can listen to it and read the book before the winter and spring sessions, when it is difficult to hold another orientation session. In chapter 8 we have provided a copy of our handout "Guidelines for Elective Leaders."

RETREATS

Our women look forward to our annual retreat. A retreat has several purposes.

• Retreats provide an opportunity for the women to nurture existing relationships and to build new ones through small and large group activities. A second and equally important purpose is to have a concentrated time of Bible teaching from a skilled Bible teacher. Third, in our world of pressure and demands, retreats provide an opportunity for reflection, restoration, and refreshment for our women.

• Many of our women invite friends and family to the retreat, knowing that they will have the opportunity to understand the message of the gospel. We always inform our retreat speaker that we will have those who do not know Christ in our group, so that she will be sure to include a presentation of the gospel.

• Retreats provide for intergenerational contact as well as an opportunity for participation for women who work outside the home to get better acquainted with those who do not.

Retreats take a great deal of careful planning and fall under the duties of the special events coordinator. She recruits committees and delegates the responsibilities of registration, skits, free time activities, and hospitality. However, the entire board participates in choosing the speaker(s) after listening to tapes. A breakdown on planning and the committees required to hold a retreat are also included in chapter 9.

SATURDAY SPECIALS

During the summer we hold two or three Saturday Specials, a one-day event complete in itself. These usually come in June and July and include Bible teaching, a missionary speaker or a book review, and three or four elective workshops. These specials provide an opportunity to keep in touch during the summer months and also expose new women to women's ministry. These specials can be included during the school year as well, especially to reach the younger, the working, and the single women in your church.

LUNCHEONS

- **A Christmas luncheon,** a mother-daughter dinner, or similar day or evening special events provide other opportunities for inviting friends and family to visit our Women's Ministries Program. A special speaker is invited by the board, and a theme is set for publicity and decorations. Sign-up sheets enlist helpers for the decorating and for kitchen help. These service opportunities provide an entry point for new people to volunteer for this limited involvement and thereby gain a sense of ownership of the ministry. Many of our board members began by helping out in these small ways. We are constantly on the lookout for interested and faithful people who are willing to serve others. Chapter 9 includes a checklist for planning a special luncheon.
- **End-of-session luncheons** add variety to the program by changing our format for the last week of each session in a number of ways.

  1. We specifically plan for the format to be a luncheon for the day group and a dinner for the evening group. (Some suggestions for menus are found near the end of chapter 9, in the section "Finishing Well.")
  2. The program on the day of the luncheon is different as well. We may or may not have the full Bible lesson. We sometimes have a speaker from one of our outreach ministries, for example, Crisis Pregnancy Center, share its ministry. Or sometimes we have some of our own women report on their recent missions trips.

3. We do not meet in the elective groups that day, but rather use that time for women to give testimonies about what their electives have meant to them. Sometimes we set up tables to display the various crafts or projects made during the electives.

4. The teachers for the upcoming session present a brief preview of their classes. One of our favorite programs provides a question-and-answer time from the Bible teacher. Each week a box is available for anonymous questions, and this question-and-answer session provides an opportunity to cover a number of those.

5. Special music and an extended opportunity for fellowship make this session enjoyable. We extend the nursery time these days and ask the mothers to bring a sack lunch for their children.

The end-of-session luncheon (or dinner) proves to be a good time to invite women who don't usually come to Women's Ministries, just to whet their appetite. We also use this time to verbally express appreciation to each elective leader and to give each one a small gift.

Your church facilities affect your ability to include some of the things I have mentioned, but I find women to be incredibly creative in planning events and programs that provide warmth and fellowship under many differing circumstances. Hopefully, examples will simply stimulate your own creativity. It is your ministry.

SPECIAL MUSIC

Music speaks to the heart and the emotions. Special music provides an opportunity to prepare the women to receive God's Word. It serves almost as an emotional glue, stimulating feelings of fellowship, love, reverence, joy, peace, adoration, humility, and awe. Beautiful poetry set to music often expresses our emotions in ways that would not be possible through spoken words alone. It focuses our attention. Music is a wonderful way for more women to share their gifts and talents with the group.

An Effective Women's Ministries Program Provides Support Groups

Many women feel isolated today. Some are badly damaged from their background or in their present situations. We must face the reality that those things going on in the world are also happening in the church. Women you sit next to have been victims of incest and child abuse. Some have had abortions. Some have discovered that their husbands are homosexuals. Some have husbands divorce them for another woman.

Some are having affairs with other men. Some are struggling in very difficult marriages. Some struggle with addictions such as alcohol. We started our support group program with an elective using the spiritual twelve-step program one of our women was trained to use. Since then, that group has met regularly on another day.

Detailed information about support groups is given in chapter 10, Appendix 3, and Appendix 4. The list below gives some of support groups offered by Northwest Bible Church.

- Abortion Recovery
- Cancer Support: "Uplifters" and "CanSupport"
- Care Givers
- Divorce Recovery Group
- Hand-in-Hand (Widows' Support Group)
- Infertility
- Marriage Enrichment
- Mom-to-Mom
- New Mothers
- Twelve-Step Study Group

As you can see, variety is an ever-developing aspect of the creative ability of women to respond to others and to our culture.

An Effective Women's Ministries Program Encourages Outreach

A failure to reach out to others in our community would condemn the ministry to eventual self-destruction. Missions begins at home and extends around the world. We are committed to providing our women opportunities to serve in the church and in the community. Outreach has become an extensive part of our ministry and developed even more after our basic program was well established. Outreach ministries provide a place where some of our older women who have been faithful and involved in missions outreach for years can plug into the overall Women's Ministries Program.

We send tapes of our weekly Bible studies to all the women missionaries our church supports. We also take interest in special missions projects, personally and financially. We help support women on short term missions trips to other countries, such as Romania and the former Soviet Union. We help sponsor many of our young people as well.

At our annual, weeklong missions conference, we invite women missionaries to speak about missions from a woman's point of view. This exposes our women to world missions, and for many it is their first personal encounter with those involved in international missions.

In addition, our women have been involved in a multitude of local outreach programs since we began the Women's Ministries. Each year new opportunities surface; one outreach may replace another as we grow, expand, and adapt. The list below gives some of the outreach programs that have proved effective for us, as well as some suggestions to stimulate your own thinking. Chapter 10, Appendix 3, and Appendix 4 give more detailed information.

- Captain Casserole
- Church Office or Library Assistance
- Citizens' Awareness Table
- Crisis Pregnancy Center (CPC)
- Evening Bible Study for Business and Professional Women
- Homeless Outreach
- Hospital Visitation
- Marriage Enrichment
- Newcomers
- Nursing Homes
- Sharing Closet
- Special Missions Projects
- Special Needs Children
- Tutoring Ministry

Our foreign missionary women affirm the encouragement of the Women's Ministries outreach to them. Below are several letters expressing their appreciation for the impact of this ministry.

My husband, children and I live in a small village that is 100 percent Muslim. At present we are learning the language and are in the early stages of Bible translation. The government does not know we are doing this, otherwise we would be asked to leave! Therefore, my husband has to hold a secular job, which has been teaching English, but now he has permission to do full-time "linguistic research." We have three small children: 3½-year-old twins, a boy and a girl, and a 1½-year-old girl.

With this background, I would like to tell you how much I enjoy the cassette tapes of your Bible teaching that NWB sends me. After listening to the series on Hebrews, I wondered, "Who is this who can speak directly to me on the other side of the world?" The highlight of my week is to put the kids down for a nap and listen to your tapes. What you say seems, often, to apply to me even though I'm in a foreign country living a different lifestyle from women in the U.S. What a blessing you must be to the women in Dallas. And what an encouragement you are to those of us with young children. At one point (or maybe several) of wondering why I am here in this strange culture with little children, not understanding the language or the customs (people), you reminded me that my feelings are normal and that this is a special time, not only for my children, but for me. It is also good to be reminded that as Christians we are all foreigners, even in our own country.

The main reason I am writing to you is to ask a favor! I used to teach Bible Study in English to internationals living in Milan. All of the ladies have since moved away, mostly to the States where they have found good churches. My closest friend from the study is married to an Italian, and they now live in a villa outside Florence. Her husband is very hostile to her faith, even to the point of continually throwing out her Bible if he finds her hiding places! This has gone on for years. It is hard for her to get to church on Sundays since there are none closer than thirty to forty minutes drive.

So her main fellowship is a women's Bible study at an Anglican church near her town. She began to attend in the hope that she might provide some good biblical input. There are a couple of other strong believers in it, too. I had given her a series of your tapes, and she promptly took them to the study—and the girl leading it had never heard anything like them! So, basically, you are having a tape ministry in Italy. They keep asking for more tapes. They have just about cleaned me out of just about everything that the church has sent me for the last few years and are asking for more. Could you get someone to send me another set of the Hebrews series, "Winning God's Approval"? I'm sending them the sermon tapes as well from the church services, but they like the ones from a woman particularly!

After reading a letter from one of our missionaries who was experiencing a particularly difficult time, several of our women wrote to her and called by phone with words of love and encouragement. This letter came as a result of their ministry to her:

* * * * * * * * * * * * * * *

I guess many of those sisters who heard my letter prayed for me because I feel much stronger now. Sometimes I feel tempted to write only about the bright side of the ministry, but transparency brings encouragement and prayer from the body, like a stream of red blood cells.

* * * * * * * * * * * * * * *

With the exploding availability of e-mail worldwide, a ministry of encouragement through this medium can be effectively developed and included in the outreach of your ministry. One young woman I know discovered a Web site, www.icq.com, where she and her friend serving in Papua New Guinea could "chat" real time on their keyboards. They chose a time when the missionary's young children were napping, and encouraged one another via the Internet. Technology needs to be captured in ways like this for kingdom purposes.

An Effective Women's Ministries Program Encourages Personal Friendships

Women are longing for friendships with other women. James Dobson reminds us that the loneliness and isolation women feel today is not because men have changed in the last century. Rather it is because of the breakdown in communication between women. With the increased mobility of people and the breakdown of the extended family, women's natural opportunities for relationships have been greatly curtailed.

In previous generations women did things together—cooked, sewed, quilted, canned, raised children, and mostly talked. We have largely lost that sense of community, and today the church must step in and assist women to get to know and love each other, filling the gap left by the disappearing extended family. Serving on committees and boards together, taking an elective together, going on retreats, praying together—all provide opportunities for friendships to develop. Fellowship is more than coffee and cake; it is working together toward a common goal.

Here at Northwest Bible Church we also have developed a program of intergenerational friendships called Heart-to-Heart. This program has done much to promote honest, caring friendships among our women. Details about how to implement this program, along with forms needed, are included in chapter 11 and Appendix 6.

An Effective Women's Ministries Program Remains Flexible and Relevant

A Women's Ministries program supported by church leadership provides a protective umbrella under which its activities can function. In that way there are not many independent and overlapping things going on with no central coordination or focus. There is accountability, which is essential. Of course, our ministry did not begin with all of the programs just outlined. Many were suggested or added as needs surfaced and as people were available to implement them. At their request I met with a core group to organize an evening class for businesswomen that discussed the issues women face in the marketplace. Our approach for new ministries has been first to find a leader, then to work with her in setting goals and guidelines. I told this group that we had only two basic requirements. One, they were part of the Women's Ministries program and thus accountable to us, and two, their lessons needed to be based on Scripture. With those basics in mind, they were free to do whatever would meet their needs.

Another woman called and said she would like to organize a support group for women caring for aging parents. I told her to pursue it and we would help organize it. This group has been a great encouragement to women at that stage in life. We also started a support group for widows. They call themselves Hand-in-Hand.

As you can see, only the creativity and size of your group limit the possibilities.

Summary

As you begin to pray and plan, assess your particular situation along the lines of the twelve characteristics of an effective Women's Ministries Program. Use the questions following this chapter to begin to focus on your areas of strength and the areas where you need development.

Questions for Study and Discussion

1. Review the twelve elements of an effective Women's Ministries Program.

   a. List the features that are presently part of your ministry for women. Based on this chapter, can you think of ways of improving them?

   b. List the areas of your ministry to women that need development. Can you think of women who could be effective leaders for these new programs?

2. Which of the elements of an effective Women's Ministries Program seem particularly relevant to your situation, and why?

3. When and where do you think you could begin?

4. List five specific ways to pray about your plans.

Five

ASSESSING
THE CULTURE

Evaluating your specific and individual ministry situation and developing a biblical philosophy uniquely crafted to your women has been our focus up to this point. Now to broaden the context surrounding your ministry in the twenty-first century, it will be essential to consider the broader culture.

The Impact of Culture on Your Women

This generation can be very fickle. Ours is not a culture where loyalty is deemed a virtue. If they "don't get something out of it," women will just go somewhere else. *Commitment* to friends, marriage, and church no longer comes easily or naturally for most. Many of this generation are cynical and distrust institutions such as the "organized church." They are *secular*—much less involved with religion than their parents. Over 30 percent of adults live alone. But even for those living with someone, psychologists have invented such terms as "crowded loneliness" and "living together loneliness" to describe this culture's need for fellowship and intimacy. Additionally they are easily distracted—and there are multiple distractions: TV, DVDs, and video games. People have short attention spans, live at a fast pace, and have a lack of discipline. Spectators, not participants, as Kerby Anderson of PROBE ministries describes them.

These multifaceted cultural pressures must significantly affect your planning for a Women's Ministries Program. Although the feminist movement produced some positive results, numerous negative ones as well substantially impact young women today.

Many have been indoctrinated with the idea that personal worth is found only in competing with men in the marketplace. Homemaking and mothering skills have been devalued, so the woman who chooses to stay home and care for her children often feels guilty for doing so and enjoying it. She faces challenging questions from those who do not choose to stay at home, and she is often caricatured by the mass media as mindless.

Consequently, those necessary skills, which many of us older women learned at our mother's side in previous generations, have not been transmitted to this generation. Many young women received no training in how to manage a home, cook nutritious meals, live on a cash basis within their income, nor do any of the things such as sewing and knitting that women of earlier generations learned almost automatically.

From the sixties forward affluence and national optimism led to parental indulgence. A generation of entitlement ("I have it coming to me") demands personal freedom, self-expression, and self-fulfillment as a constitutional right; it values choice and variety. Trends toward smaller families and more and more two-income families have become the norm.

During the 1950s, in over 70 percent of the homes, the husband was the breadwinner and the wife was home with the children. In our new millennium this pattern reverses to the point where only 30 percent of families fall into that formerly traditional pattern. Sixty-eight percent of women with children under six are in the workforce today. That figure continues to grow at an astonishing rate.

These women must be the church's target audience. Understanding and appreciating their needs provides ways of meeting them. Insisting on old methods results in failure and frustration for all involved. How aware are you and those you work with in developing your ministry of this impact of our present culture on your women?

On the other hand, we must not toss out good methods that effectively ministered to older generations. Somehow we must incorporate methods and styles that provide something for all. In evangelism we should use every method to reach the unbeliever; in discipleship we cannot compromise biblical standards to accommodate what the world says we must do—but we can adapt our methods to become more effective.

An effective Women's Ministries Program is really evangelism and discipleship at many levels simultaneously. Ministry such as this challenges a woman's creativity and blesses her in many ways. A Women's Ministries Program serves effectively as an umbrella spanning the activities needed for young and old, new and mature believers. A Women's Ministries Board accountable to church leadership, yet with the authority to plan, promote, and implement programs, provides a most practical way to proceed. It will relieve the pastor and male staff of a burden they are unable to carry alone.

Recognize the Distortion
of Sexual Relationships Today

In 2000 some 5.5 million couples lived together without marriage. With the rising acceptance of extramarital sex, men do not find it necessary to make a commitment to a woman. This pressure on young women needs to be addressed regularly from the Scripture. Many of these couples come to church on Sunday and participate as part of your congregation. This troublesome undercurrent of sexual license affects the way you develop the content for your particular ministry. The understanding and support of an older woman encourages young women to maintain a life of purity.

The sexual relationship is frequently viewed as a right open to all rather than the privilege reserved for the protection of marriage. Purity and self-restraint run against the prevailing flow of culture and practice of upcoming generations. Titus 2 makes clear that older women are to teach younger women the importance of purity, and this relates specifically to a healthy understanding of God's gift of the sexual relationship

The church must reach this media-saturated generation and their children. We will most effectively reach them as we recognize their characteristics and provide ways to attract them. Insisting on old methods will end in failure. Consider how the following characteristics of this generation might impact your ministry; some will help you and some will present challenges for you to overcome:

- Places a priority on personal relationships
- Appreciates and demands diversity
- Sees change as good, not bad; is easily bored
- Cannot always count on family for support
- Does not believe in absolutes
- Believes there are many roads to God
- Feels free to express negative emotions
- Prefers short-term commitments
- Believes the Existential philosophy "You only go around once."

Consider the Unique Needs
of Single and Career Women

The enormous growth in the number of singles living alone presents additional challenges. Their number includes those never married, the widowed, and the divorced. Single parent families increase every year, and economically these are often the most disadvantaged in our society. No one can measure the damage divorce has wreaked on the children—and these children are the parents of upcoming generations.

How do we minister to singles? This concern increases continually in the local church. Over one-third of my home church is single; therefore, we have a Minister to Singles and a strong singles ministry. I recognize that frequently smaller churches do not. However, even in our singles ministry, we have found that single women still desire connection with women of the church. They are weary of associating only with their peers. Life lacks a certain reality when it lacks intergenerational connectedness. Single women also have many questions, questions that require the counsel of older, spiritually mature women. Consider these questions I was asked when invited to meet with a small group of Christian single women:

1. Can you offer encouragement for women who have not had the example of a Christ-centered marriage in their homes that their own marriages can be different, and how can women learn to recognize when their relationships are following the unhealthy patterns they learned as children?
2. Define submission and describe how we are to apply it in the following situations:
   a. with men at work
   b. with men friends
   c. in our church
   d. in dating relationships
   e. with Christian versus non-Christian men
3. What are our natural instincts and desires as women? How can we constructively deal with those desires in our current position as single women? How can we be content?
4. How should we handle the situation when a single friend becomes pregnant?
5. When we are interested in a dating relationship, is there an appropriate way to pursue it?
6. If we have already given up our virginity, is there any way we can be pure again before God, and how can we deal with the guilt that may be involved?
7. What kind of ministry options are appropriate and available to single women?
8. Can a divorced woman have a ministry in the church?

Because we offer an evening program, many of our singles and career women teach electives. They are been involved in outreach and missions. They are generous in their giving to special projects, and they love the Heart-to-Heart relationships, both as Juniors and Seniors. (This program is described in detail in chapter 11.) The abilities that have made them successful in business can be tapped for use in the family of God. That's why I'm so thrilled to see some of them take the initiative to form an evening class for business and professional women.

We also have to recognize that the number of single parents, especially single mothers, is increasing. We in the church can do much to help, and we need to find creative ways to do that. For instance, our Men's Ministry recently had a workday where several groups of men went to the homes of single mothers and widows to do repairs and yard work. The Heart-to-Heart Friendships have worked here, as well.

Give Your Program an
Umbrella of Protection and Accountability

A Women's Ministries Program serves as an umbrella for the activities needed for young and old, new and mature believers, providing protection and accountability. The Women's Ministries Board is accountable to church leadership but enjoys delegated authority to plan, promote, and implement programs. This structure is really the only practical way to go. Often this can free the pastor and male staff to concentrate on the development of male leadership.

Part Three

BREAKING
GROUND

When a farmer plows for planting,
does he plow continually?
Does he keep on breaking up
and harrowing the soil?

ISAIAH 28:24

Six

DEVELOPING
A DESIGN

We discovered from Scripture that women are qualified for ministry and called to ministry. You have begun to make an assessment of your present situation and consider our present culture. Now you can begin to develop a design suited to your unique circumstances, drawing together the various aspects of a Women's Ministries Program and applying it to your own church.

I often hear the question, "But our church is not a big church like yours. How can we do what you do?" My response—just scale the program to fit your resources. Your Women's Ministries Board may be smaller—just big enough to cover your activities. You don't have to begin with three sessions. Start with one in the fall and one in the spring. Have six-week sessions, or even less. Have a good, relevant Bible study, and then offer three or four electives, depending on their variety. Pair up women in teaching teams. Have an elective that is a potpourri of crafts, so that if a person is good at only one or two things, she will still be able to share these skills. We had a very successful elective on how to have family devotions. The leaders invited a different guest speaker each week, and each one had something different to offer. We do this in counselor training, cooking, crafts, and other electives. Be creative! Adapt to what you have in personnel and facilities. If your church does not have adequate room, you may be able to use some homes near the church for your small groups.

"Heart-to-Heart," our program of matching Juniors and Seniors described in detail in chapter 11, provides another good place for a smaller church to begin. Creating an opportunity for deepening intergenerational relationships can develop the core team needed to develop a full program of women's ministries.

Surveying the Needs

Now to begin designing your own program, you need to evaluate your individual situation. This chapter is intended to support you and your committee through this process as you correlate the varied aspects of women's ministries outlined in earlier chapters. Use this outline as a working tool to organize your thoughts and evaluations, incorporating the uniqueness of your situation as you move through the process. Also included in this chapter are some practical suggestions regarding contacting and securing outside speakers as well as assistance in dealing with some special problems.

But please note—these ideas are just suggestions, a beginning track to run on. Be creative. Add to it. Expand it. Change it. Give your plan a unique style that fits your group yet encompasses the basic, biblical principles discussed previously

As you develop your own Women's Ministries Program, you may be find it helpful to keep in mind the various thoughts and suggestions given in this chapter. The assessment form on pages 85–89 will be useful also.

Child Care

Essential to an effective and successful program is good child care. Often child care is considered something the women must provide or do for themselves, yet that demand puts a burden on the very young women we are trying to impact. The mother of young children who can't afford to pay for child care each week for several children simply won't come. Then we as a ministry lose this significant opportunity and one we are commanded to fulfill. Additionally, if child care is manned by volunteers, whose ranks are filled with those already caring daily for little ones, we find they often drop out.

Child care is a legitimate need, as much as are facilities and utilities. Secure paid workers. Many women welcome the extra money and will commit themselves for the year. Retired women on Social Security make wonderful workers. But ideally, the church would consider this as its investment in their young families and provide for it in the overall church budget. I recognize that a lot of re-education may be involved to accomplish this objective.

Special Speakers

We often invite women from outside our fellowship to speak for special events, such as retreats or luncheons. We want to be sensitive to their needs and demonstrate appreciation for the investment of their time as they come to share their gifts with us.

We begin by securing recommendations of effective speakers from various sources (other churches, ministries, and recommendations from the pastor.) We try to get an

DESIGN FOR _____
(Name of your church)

I.   Prayer Group
Participants:

Pastor's wife: _____

Others: _____

_____

_____

Place: _____

Date: _____

Time: _____

Frequency: _____

Specific requests: _____

Develop a sample survey: _____

Draft survey completed: _____ date

Final survey completed: _____ date

II. Appointment with Your Pastor
Date: _____   Time: _____

Convey concerns: _____

_____

_____

_____

Request input: _____

_____

_____

Show him the sample survey: _____

_____

Request to survey women in the congregation:

Date(s): _____

Method: _____

_____

(Prefer a method that reaches as many of your women as possible. Perhaps included in a Sunday bulletin for several weeks, an e-mail memo, or a combination of several ways.)

Ask your pastor for his suggestions of other interested women: _____

_____

III. **Refine and Finalize the Survey Form**

Completion date: _____

Survey date: _____

Pastoral or other approval: _____

IV. **Distribute Surveys and Compile Results**

Develop a list of your greatest needs: _____

_____

_____

_____

_____

_____

How can you meet those needs (develop goals)? _____

_____

_____

_____

_____

_____

V. **Evaluation and Design of the New Program**

What kind of program now exists? _____

What kind of program are you recommending? _____

_____

_____

_____

Target date to begin: _____

How will you handle the following programming elements?

    Frequency: _____

    Day/Evening: _____

    Child care: _____

    Finances: _____

    Leadership: _____

    Teaching: _____

    Recruitment: _____

    Presentation to church leadership: _____

    _____

What board positions are needed to accomplish your goals?

(Job descriptions are given in chapter 7.)

_____

_____

_____

Who will serve on your first Women's Ministries Board?

_____

_____

_____

Target date for presentation to leadership: _____

VI.   **Specific Plans to Move Ahead After Board Approval**

Subject for the first series: _____ _____

_____

Number of sessions: _____ Day of the week: _____

Time: _____ Bible teacher: _____

Electives to be offered: _____

_____

_____

_____

_____

_____

_____

Brochure preparation for the series (see Appendix 5 for examples): _____

_____

_____

_____

_____

The kind of kickoff event (i.e., luncheon, coffee, dinner): _____

_____

The date and time for the kickoff event: _____

_____

VII.   **Kickoff Event for the New Program**
       Speaker who can motivate women ministering to women: _____

       _____

       Invite the pastor to welcome the women: _____

       Posters: _____

       Skits:_____

       Other details: _____

       _____

       _____

       _____

       _____

       Hand out brochures and answer questions: _____

       _____

VIII. **Conduct the First Series**
       Subject: _____   Bible teacher: _____
       Dates: _____   Day and time: _____

       _____

       Hand out evaluation sheets: _____

IX.   **Evaluation and Appreciation of the First Series**
       Notes of appreciation to the participants: _____
       Luncheon of appreciation for elective leaders: _____

Review surveys: _____

_____

_____

_____

Areas for improvement: _____

_____

_____

_____

New people who were involved: _____

_____

_____

_____

Potential leadership: _____

_____

_____

New series: _____

Bible teacher: _____

Dates: _____   Number of weeks: _____

Electives: _____

_____

_____

_____

Other: _____

_____

_____

_____

* * * * * * * * * * * * * * * * *

audiotape of something the speaker has done previously. If possible, we secure this audiotape and listen to it before we even make a first contact. If that is not possible, we graciously request a tape of some message the person has presented.

In making this request, however, we try to avoid the kind of attitude demonstrated in the following excerpt from a letter I received regarding a speaking engagement:

We are making a composite list of women speakers for future church retreats, etc. We would appreciate your sending a résumé of your ministry, listing any teaching, lecturing, or speaking engagements you may have done. An audiocassette of one of your speaking engagements, a copy of your theological doctrine, and specific details of fees charged would be helpful.

Try to remember that the person you are contacting *did not apply* for the opportunity with your ministry. Rather, you are asking her to come and share her ministry with you, so your first contact must be gracious, not demanding.

Generally your first contact is by phone. If we have listened to the tape and wish to invite the speaker, we are ready to find out if the date of our retreat or seminar might be open on her calendar. If it is, we need to cover the points below in a natural conversation. The points of this outline may help you begin to secure special speakers.

1. Give the speaker a little background on your group, the age span, and how many participants you expect. Give her your name and telephone number.

2. Discuss possible subjects for the event, asking if she already has some messages prepared. Ask her if she would be willing for you to tape the messages for those who cannot attend.

3. Determine if she charges a set fee, or if she would be able to work within your budget for speakers. That budget should cover all her expenses, including airfare, and would allow at least $150 per message. It is important to realize that a retreat speaker invests from two to three days of personal time to minister to your group—and you do not want to ask her to contribute involuntarily to your ministry. Find out if she prefers to make her own travel arrangements, or if she prefers for you to do so. You can call to remind her nearer to the retreat date to secure advance purchase tickets. (For more on this subject, see "Giving Speakers a Tangible Sign of Appreciation" later in this chapter)

4. If you plan to have small, breakout groups at a retreat, usually following the messages, ask the speaker to send you either discussion questions or appropriate subjects in order for you to compile them. It would be helpful to give her the date prior to the retreat by which you need them.

5. Ask the speaker for any special needs she might have, such as lapel mikes or overhead projector. Ask her how you as a committee might be praying for her as you approach your time together. If the event is other than a retreat, ask what type of accommodations she prefers, i.e., a hotel or a private home. Ask your speaker if she has any special diet needs or any other special needs that you might be able to accommodate. Be sure that the accommodations provide a comfortable atmosphere with privacy for study.

6. Give her an idea of the type of clothing appropriate for the event—casual, dressy banquet, and so on.
7. Ask her if she is willing to counsel individually should there be those who desire it and if time permits.
8. Confirm your conversation with a letter detailing the items you discussed.

COURTESY TO THE SPEAKER AT THE EVENT

1. Treat the speaker as you would a welcome guest in your home.
2. Make arrangements for someone to meet her (pick her up at the airport) and to sit with her and introduce her to others. Providing a special hostess like this makes her comfortable and provides a great task for a young, enthusiastic committee member.
3. Secure a private room and bath at the retreat. Most conference centers have rooms especially for the speakers.
4. Provide a basket of fruit or flowers in her room as a special welcome.
5. Thank her verbally from the front, giving opportunity for appreciation. Give her the honorarium check privately before she leaves.

FOLLOW-UP WITH THE SPEAKER

1. A written thank-you is always appreciated, especially if it includes some comments and feedback regarding God's use of her, as well as specific lessons or portions that were particularly helpful or meaningful. In this way you have a reciprocal ministry to her future effectiveness.
2. Continue to pray for her ministry and the fruit of it in your group.

GIVING SPEAKERS A TANGIBLE SIGN OF APPRECIATION

When you invite a woman to teach a Bible study or speak at a retreat or at any of your meetings, you should thank her in a tangible way. At Northwest Bible Church we do not pay people who attend this church for whatever service they do here. That represents their ministry to their own church family. However, we do show them our appreciation with a gift of some kind—flowers, a quality piece of china or crystal, or perhaps a framed verse in calligraphy. We also send a thank-you note as well as offer personal thanks.

But when we invite someone to come from another church or place to speak or teach, we pay their expenses and give them an honorarium—a check (1 Corinthians 9:11; Galatians 6:6). There is an archaic idea that a woman doesn't need to be paid since she is supported by her husband. There should be no connection between the two. A laborer is worthy of her hire. When we consider the time invested in preparation before coming and the time taken from the speaker's own life to travel and serve us, it would be most ungracious of us to not acknowledge her service tangibly. Money for the honorarium should be included in your yearly budget or added to the cost of the occasion, for example, a luncheon ticket. If the speaker does not want to accept the money, that is her choice, but we should offer it. She should not be forced to contribute to our ministry. Let's not be stingy. God will supply the money if we give generously.

Once I was invited to speak at a kickoff luncheon for a church some distance from my home. Besides my preparation time, the event took all of my Saturday morning and part of the afternoon. When I arrived, they pinned a little corsage on me and had a little book at my place. I appreciated them. What I didn't realize was that they were all they had planned to give the speaker. I waited for a couple of weeks, then called the director of their women's ministry.

I said, "Linda, this is a little awkward for me, but I wondered if you have a policy of not giving your speakers an honorarium?"

"We give them a little gift," she replied.

I continued, "A gift is appropriate if the speaker is from your own church. But when you invite someone from elsewhere, you should plan to cover their traveling expenses and their time and effort."

She received my suggestion graciously, and about two weeks later I received a very kind letter thanking me for calling her attention to a grave oversight. There was also a satisfactory check included. Many times this issue is simply due to a lack of experience, and her teachable response encouraged me.

Special Problems You May Encounter

MAJORITY OLDER OR YOUNGER

What about a church where there are mostly older women? How do you attract younger women? If you offer a program with a Bible study addressing relevant life issues and offering electives of interest to younger women, they will come when you invite them. This can be a wonderful outreach in your neighborhood or at your office. We have women who come because they were invited by a neighbor, a fellow garden club enthusiast, or a friend at the office. They came to know the Lord or grow in their faith as a result. When they experience the benefits of relationships with these older women, they become committed to the Women's Ministries Program and start to serve as well. Older women will draw them like metal filings to a magnet.

But what about a church comprised of mostly young women under forty? In that case, the pastor's wife and the wives of the elders and deacons may have to assume the role of the older woman. You need to personally recruit any older women you do have. Don't simply announce this need, but personally seek them out and speak to them, urging them to invest in the lives of many younger women interested in mentors. Help these older women sense your desire for their involvement. And remember, you can't accomplish it all in one year. This must be a process of ongoing development. We at Northwest Bible Church keep changing and improving our program each year, but we continually keep our long-range goals in mind. We want to meet needs, develop maturity and leadership in our women, and equip them to serve.

WHEN LEADERSHIP IS NOT SUPPORTIVE

This can be a very challenging problem. Sometimes the leadership is not supportive because the men sincerely believe that women should not have any positions of leadership at all. They take the passages that set limits on women (1 Corinthians 14:35 and 1 Timothy 2:11–14) and then apply them to every area of life, though they refer only to the public worship service. That is poor interpretation of Scripture. But it is difficult to overcome because it feeds a natural desire of many men to control. However, you will not accomplish anything by becoming militant and demanding your rights. Gather a couple of other women and share your vision. Include the pastor's wife if she is open. Begin with prayer, especially for proceeding with a right spirit, patience, and wisdom, and for protection from a critical spirit.

Then you might start by approaching your pastor on the basis of Titus 2, where Paul instructs Titus, the pastor, to teach the older women so they can teach the younger. Ask him if he would teach a group of mature women who want to obey God's command. He might be willing to do this or provide for it to be done. It has been exciting to me to see women who have been sent to us by their pastors and churches to learn about a Women's Ministries Program, with their expenses paid by their church.

In a church where you have a program in need of change, you might do as our women did. Investigate, gather evidence, survey your own women. Plan a program that will meet your needs and suit your situation. Then approach your leadership. Speak to the pastor. Share your concern with an elder or deacon who may be sympathetic. Invite the Elder or Deacon Board to dinner. Be organized and factual as you present your proposal. Trust the Lord to change minds and hearts in His time.

But if the male leadership is not supportive, don't give up. Start a small Bible study in someone's home and invite friends and neighbors. Have a craft day in another home. Ask God to give you creative ways to obey Him, even beginning with a one-on-one relationship. Choose not to be a source of dissension in the church. You will be tempted to complain. Resist that temptation; your response will be observed. God may grant you men with changed minds, or He may change the men in leadership. These are all possibilities. But we have seen that when leadership sees the blessings a responsible Women's Ministries Program brings to the whole church, they are supportive and enthusiastic. Frequently, elders have told me personally or written notes expressing appreciation for what the Women's Ministries Program means to the church and to their own wives. Elders' and deacons' wives can be your biggest allies.

Let me add a word about the pastor's wife. Very often, she is the one with the vision to start and lead a Women's Ministries Program, and her interest is important, necessary, and effective. She should always be involved with the women of the church, and women love to have her participation. But as soon as someone else is capable of replacing her, it's a good idea for her to relinquish the leadership and continue to serve in another capacity. That way the pastor and his wife are protected from the criticism that they run everything. The responsibility of leadership is to equip others to serve, not to do it all ourselves.

When you have a denominational women's program existing, you have a special challenge. You can try to work within that structure and adapt it to some of the ideas you have gleaned from this workbook. You can suggest changes at your regional and national meetings. I have opportunity to speak at some of those conferences, and I always find interest in improving the denominational program. Methods should not be set in stone. If you can't introduce change without upsetting the applecart, then supplement the program with Saturday Specials or with a six-week Bible study or counseling course. Have a craft day. Take on a new outreach to the community. Start a clothes closet for the needy in your church and community. Form a support group for young mothers, or cancer sufferers. Branch out. You will always find someone with a special interest who can carry the ball for you. All of these ideas will allow relationships to flourish.

Always keep your priorities in order. Bible study should be first and foremost because that produces spiritual growth and the motivation necessary to serve. Then you need variety to tap all the resources available to you and to equip women in all the areas where they have responsibilities. Encourage friendships; be available for counseling. Let God stretch you. No one is adequate in herself for this, but God is the one who makes us adequate and competent. He just wants your willing heart. He will work through you.

Now that we have looked at these considerations, it's time for you to dig in for yourself.

Seven

CREATING A
WOMEN'S
MINISTRY BOARD

When planning a new project around our homes or in the garden, most of us enjoy perusing slick magazines full of colorful pictures and creative ideas. We gain inspiration and stimulation for our unique project. This chapter and chapters 8–11 are offered to accomplish that purpose. In them you will find detailed information about the various components of the Women's Ministries Program at Northwest Bible Church in Dallas, Texas. We give you this information not because we think our way is the only way, or even the best way. However, it is an example of how one church set up a program.

We begin this chapter with an organizational chart of our Women's Ministries Board at Northwest Bible Church. Then we give a complete job description for each of our ten board positions.

We hope that these work sheets will give you inspiration and direction and provide a helpful springboard to take your group to even greater creativity. But bear in mind—we have been developing our program over a number of years. Yours will take time also. Let the ideas in this chapter stimulate your thinking. You may want to take these sheets and simply highlight the sections you feel are applicable to your present situation. Exercise the creative skills enjoyed by all women as you adapt them to fit the unique situation in your own church.

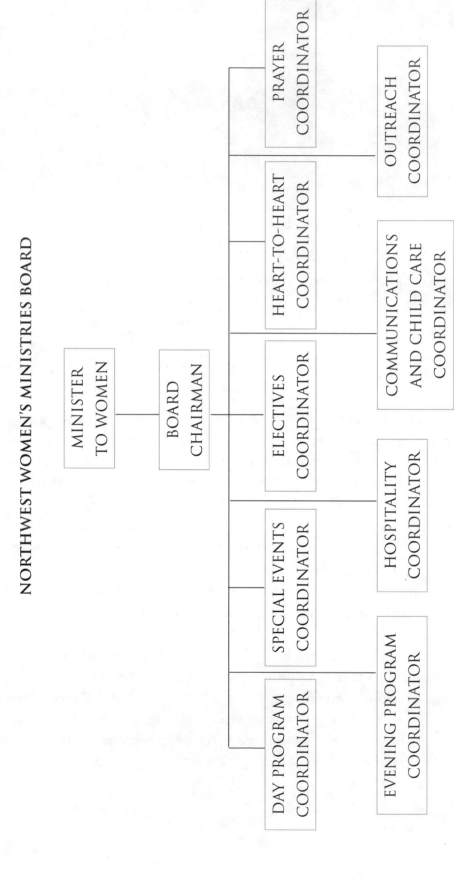

NORTHWEST WOMEN'S MINISTRIES BOARD

MINISTER TO WOMEN

BOARD CHAIRMAN

DAY PROGRAM COORDINATOR

SPECIAL EVENTS COORDINATOR

ELECTIVES COORDINATOR

HEART-TO-HEART COORDINATOR

PRAYER COORDINATOR

EVENING PROGRAM COORDINATOR

HOSPITALITY COORDINATOR

COMMUNICATIONS AND CHILD CARE COORDINATOR

OUTREACH COORDINATOR

JOB DESCRIPTIONS

MINISTER TO WOMEN

Reporting relationship: The associate pastor and the elder board
Primary function: To oversee the Women's Ministries Program

RESPONSIBILITIES

Ministry to women
1. Plan, promote, and coordinate weekly a Women's Ministries Program for Tuesday mornings and Wednesday evenings (September–May)
2. Prepare and teach Bible lessons Tuesdays and Wednesdays
3. Meet regularly with the Women's Ministries Board
4. Assist members of the board in accomplishing their responsibilities
5. Recruit new Women's Ministries Board members
6. Recruit Bible teachers
7. Help recruit leaders for the elective classes
8. Coordinate training for support counseling ministry
9. Carry out discipleship and leadership development
10. Provide personal counseling on request
11. Prepare and administer the Women's Ministries budget
12. Speak to individual groups as requested, for example, singles, young mothers, youth
13. Hospital visitation
14. Supervise women interns from Dallas Theological Seminary
15. Supervise and participate in the yearly retreat and other special events
16. Supervise Saturday Specials in the summer
17. Supervise and approve all ministries for women in the church and for women in the community, among which may be:
    a. Crisis Pregnancy Center
    b. Breast cancer support group
    c. Care givers (lay counseling)
    d. Abortion recovery
    e. Homeless and battered women shelters
    f. Mom-to-Mom (young mothers' support)

g. Professional women's group

h. Widows' support group

18. Monthly Bible study with support staff women

Coordination with the staff and elder board

1. Attend weekly staff meetings

2. Report weekly to the associate pastor

3. Report in writing and in person to the Elder Board as requested

Other responsibilities:

1. Assist other churches in starting Women's Ministries Programs, offering suggestions by phone, letter, and personal interviews.

2. Frequently speak in other church meetings and retreats

3. Serve as Visiting Lecturer in the Women's Ministries course at Dallas Theological Seminary

---

WOMEN'S MINISTRIES BOARD CHAIRMAN

Reporting relationship: Minister to Women

Primary function: To chair the Women's Ministries Board and to advise and assist the Minister to Women when the board is not in session

RESPONSIBILITIES

1. Chair the meetings of the Women's Ministries Board

2. See that each member of the board is functioning in her area of responsibility

3. Plan the times and agendas of the meetings; arrange for recording the minutes of the meetings

4. Provide a calendar of events and meeting dates for each member

5. Be responsible for keeping the board informed between meetings

6. Meet regularly with the Minister to Women when the board is not in session

7. Plan the agendas for the Tuesday meetings and make announcements and/or prepare announcements to be given to elective leaders

8. Appoint a secretary to record the minutes of board meetings

9. Support and encourage others in their positions on the board

DAY PROGRAM
COORDINATOR

Reporting relationship: Chairman of the Women's Ministries Board
Primary function: To oversee the operation of the morning program

RESPONSIBILITIES

1. See that the facility needs of the teachers are met as they have requested
2. See that the P.A. system is set up and manned and that all equipment is returned to its proper place
3. Work with the Electives Coordinator to keep in regular contact with elective leaders
4. Write a personal thank-you note to each elective leader when her teaching period is over
5. Collect and keep a record of the offering and make a date-attendance-offering chart
6. Assist the Minister to Women in the selection of a pianist and leader of music (the song time should be 9:30–9:40, with occasionally one additional song after the teacher speaks)
7. Collect and distribute the tape orders; appoint someone to sit in the foyer with tapes before and after the class to answer questions concerning the tapes
8. Take tapes, offering, and tape orders to the church office
9. Support and encourage others in their positions on the board

EVENING PROGRAM
COORDINATOR

Reporting Relationship: Chairman of the Women's Ministries Board
Primary function: To oversee the operation of the evening program

RESPONSIBILITIES

1. See that the facility needs of the teachers are met as they have requested

2. See that the P.A. equipment is set up and manned and that all equipment is returned to its proper place

3. Write a personal thank-you note to each elective leader when her teaching period is over

4. Assist the Minister to Women in the selection of a pianist and leader of music

5. Collect and distribute the tape orders

6. Be responsible for the refreshments on Wednesday evening, which could occasionally include more than coffee

7. Keep a written record of the number present each week, giving the number to the Minister to Women

8. Assist the hospitality coordinator at the end-of-session dinner

9. Be the "hostess" on Wednesday evenings, being present at the welcoming table to greet and assist ladies

10. Support and encourage others in their positions on the board

---

OUTREACH COORDINATOR

Reporting relationship: Chairman of the Women's Ministries Board
Primary function: To oversee existing outreach ministries and to organize and implement new ones as opportunities arise

RESPONSIBILITIES

1. Submit the names of possible leaders for each outreach ministry to the Minister to Women for approval before recruiting them

2. Have the leader of each outreach ministry report to her and meet with or call her at least monthly to assist and to encourage

3. Investigate new ministries and report to the board on their feasibility for the church, and update the board members at meetings

4. Be alert to opportunities that come up throughout the year that offer outreach participation

5. Coordinate the flow of information on outreach opportunities to the church and encourage participation through a variety of means: announcements, sign-up sheets, recruitment calls

6. Support and encourage others in their positions on the board

```
┌─────────────────────────────┐
│         OUTREACH            │
│       COORDINATOR           │
└─────────────────────────────┘
```

Hospital Visitation	Hand-in-Hand (widows)
Captain Casserole	New Mother Visitation
Abortion Recovery	Uplifters (cancer support group)
Help in Church Office or Library	West Dallas Ministry (tutoring inner-city students)
Ministry to Battered Women	Missions Projects
Crisis Pregnancy Center	Nursing Home Ministry
Infertility Support Group	

```
┌─────────────────────────────┐
│        HOSPITALITY          │
│       COORDINATOR           │
└─────────────────────────────┘
```

Reporting Relationship: Chairman of the Women's Ministries Board
Primary function: To coordinate the activities involving hospitality

RESPONSIBILITIES

1. Coordinate the day luncheon and the evening dinner with the Day and Evening Program Coordinators at the end of each session and select women to assist her
2. Assist the Special Events Coordinator where her responsibilities overlap with that of the Hospitality Coordinator
3. Be responsible to secure refreshments for Tuesday mornings, which usually include finger snacks
4. Be responsible for the orientation meeting for the elective leaders
5. Be responsible for selecting gifts for the elective leaders at the end of each session
6. Coordinate the luncheon for the elective leaders (table decoration and menu) held each session

7. For board meetings, provide coffee, hot water and ice water, and possibly include simple snacks
8. Provide the menu and food for the end-of-year board retreat
9. Provide the beverages and snacks for the Saturday Specials
10. Support and encourage others in their positions on the board

SPECIAL EVENTS
COORDINATOR

Reporting relationship: Chairman of the Women's Ministries Board
Primary function: To be responsible for all special programs apart from the regular weekly program, such as retreats, luncheons, and seminars

RESPONSIBILITIES

1. Select the chairman for event committees for various special events.
2. Investigate potential programs and report to the Women's Ministries Board regarding their feasibility for us (the choice of the speaker shall be a board decision)
3. As called upon, assist the Hospitality Coordinator where her responsibilities overlap with those of the Special Events Coordinator
4. Work with the Electives Coordinator to enlist elective leaders for the Saturday Specials
5. Support and encourage others in their positions on the board

ELECTIVES
COORDINATOR

Reporting Relationship: Chairman of the Women's Ministries Board
Primary function: To recruit elective leaders for each session and to act as a liaison between the Women's Ministries Board and elective leaders

RESPONSIBILITIES

1. Seek out women from the church to share their talents with the Women's Ministries Program

2. Coordinate electives each session in order to maintain variety and balance in the program
3. Obtain descriptions of the electives from the elective leaders, prepare the brochure, and give it to the church secretary to be printed
4. Assist the elective leaders in planning their room set up and in obtaining needed supplies, such as overhead projectors, a blackboard, recorders, and TV monitors; give a list of those requirements to the church secretary
5. Prior to each session, turn in room set up requirements to the secretary in charge of scheduling
6. Check to make sure that the room set up is correct
7. Contact and assess the needs of the elective leaders and communicate information from the board
8. Coordinate activities with the Special Events Coordinator for the Saturday Specials
9. Contact the elective leaders about luncheons and special information
10. Support and encourage others in their positions on the board
11. Assign individual elective leaders to Women's Ministries Board members as regular prayer partners

---

COMMUNICATIONS AND CHILD CARE COORDINATOR

Reporting relationship: Chairman of the Women's Ministries Board

Primary function: To provide for the publicity needs of the Women's Ministries Program and for child care during all Women's Ministries functions; if your church does not have a fully staffed children's department, some of these functions may need to be separated or shared with an assistant

RESPONSIBILITIES

1. Determine the number of children in the program and communicate that information to the person in charge of the nursery
2. Report back to the Women's Ministries Board concerning any needs that may arise
3. Oversee the functioning of the child care program during Women's Ministries functions

4. Be responsible for any promotion—such as posters, special fliers, or newspaper announcements—for regular activities and/or special events
5. Be responsible for placing notices in the church bulletin
6. Support and encourage others in their positions on the board

---

HEART-TO-HEART
COORDINATOR

Reporting Relationship: Chairman of the Women's Ministries Board
Primary function: To oversee the operation of the Heart-to-Heart ministry of Junior and Senior partners (see chapter 11 for greater detail about this position and ministry)

RESPONSIBILITIES

1. Select an assistant to help with administrative responsibilities
   a. To help in matching Junior/Senior partners
   b. To help make rematches when necessary
   c. To help coordinate and publicize social events
2. Select the Junior and Senior members for the Heart-to-Heart steering committee
   a. To call the matched partners for follow-up and accountability
   b. To assist in preparing for coffees, teas, social events, and announcements
3. As able, assist other churches in starting Heart-to-Heart programs
4. Support and encourage others in their positions on the board

---

PRAYER
COORDINATOR

Reporting Relationship: Chairman of the Women's Ministries Board
Primary Function: To encourage and facilitate prayer among the board as well as the ministry

RESPONSIBILITIES:

1. To work with the Electives Coordinator to assign elective leaders to board prayer partners
2. To promote a spirit of prayer in all aspects of Women's Ministries
3. To encourage electives that focus on equipping and encouraging personal and corporate prayer
4. To organize a prayer chain in Women's Ministries

Eight

OFFERING ELECTIVES

With variety the emphasis in our present generation, the electives program in any Women's Ministry Program provides this element—and is a key part of its success. This chapter gives suggestions for choosing and training elective leaders and a comprehensive list of the various electives offered over the years at Northwest Bible Church. We use the handout "Guidelines for Elective Leaders" prior to each session to train those who lead one of the small elective groups.

Securing Elective Leaders

All members of the Women's Ministries Board continually listen to program participants and seek new and beneficial electives as well as suggest women to lead them. The best methods and the ones most frequently used to secure elective leaders are personal contacts and recommendations.

Also, at the close of each session of the Women's Ministries Program, we survey the women, providing an opportunity for suggestions as well as new volunteers to help teach. (An example of such a survey follows immediately after this section.) This provides a significant entry point for new people to participate more fully if they so desire. The board considers these possibilities and acts as a clearinghouse, choosing exactly what to offer and who will lead the various electives.

Some women are comfortable sharing a skill such as sewing or cooking but are not comfortable leading the prayer and sharing aspect of the elective. In such cases we find it helpful to pair that woman with another woman more experienced in handling those functions. As they work as a team, many times the woman initially hesitant to lead the prayer and sharing becomes much more confident and develops in this area herself. Elective leadership becomes an excellent training ground for future leaders of the Women's Ministries Program.

Some electives, such as an elective concerning family devotions, cooking, or training in lay counseling, might be too varied in content to expect lessons from only one teacher. In those cases we have often found it effective to invite a different speaker for each of the six to eight sessions. In our counselor training elective, for example, we were able to invite several professional counselors to participate in one or two sessions and add their expertise without having to be there each week.

In this type of arrangement, however, it is important to have one woman who hosts and facilitates for all the meetings of that elective. She meets with the other elective leaders and handles the shepherding aspects of the class. This provides continuity and the valuable link of communication between the board and this class.

WOMEN'S MINISTRIES SURVEY

Please take the time to tell us what you'd like to have offered for the fall session.
We NEED your input, ideas, and feedback!

I attend _____ Tuesday morning   _____ Wednesday evening

What things do you particularly like about the Women's Ministries Program?

_____

_____

Is there anything you'd like to see changed about the Women's Ministries Program or
its format? _____

_____

Do you have a skill or talent that you could share with or teach to other women?

1. _____

2. _____

What other elective courses would you like to see taught?

1. _____

2. _____

Listed below are some of the classes that have been requested or suggested. Please
indicate if you would be willing to teach or team teach any of them.

_____ Gardening	_____ Needlework/crafts
_____ Floral arranging	_____ Blended families
_____ Oil/folk art painting	_____ Dealing with stress
_____ Home economy	_____ Ministry of encouragement
_____ Loss and the grief process	_____ Spiritual accountability

WAYS I CAN HELP

_____ Pass out songbooks	_____ Take offering
_____ Lead singing	_____ Work on retreat
_____ Play the piano	_____ You name it, I'm willing

Do you have any constructive suggestions that might improve the effectiveness of the
Women's Ministries Program? _____

_____

Name _____ Address _____

Phone _____ Church home _____

Is there a retreat speaker you can recommend?

_____

Where (how) might we contact her?

_____

Which location do you prefer for a retreat?   Conference Center   Area Hotel

(Circle One)

Guidelines for Elective Leaders

The elective time provides an integral part of the entire program. It is not only the means of communicating a skill but also the method of drawing people together in smaller groups to encourage their spiritual growth. For this reason an elective leader must consider herself not only a teacher but also a role model. With that in mind, here are some guidelines to enhance your leadership.

1. Arrive fifteen minutes before each session so that you can welcome your women as they arrive and set an example by being present for the beginning of the Bible study. This validates the primary role of the Bible for each session. Your presence will be a personal blessing and indicates to others the importance you place on Bible study.

2. Call the people on your list and let them know they are in your class and where the class will be meeting. Give them necessary preliminary information.

3. Keep an attendance record. Call absentees to let them know they were missed.

4. Arrange now for a substitute who can be available on short notice should you have an emergency. If you know you cannot be there on a specific date, arrange for a teacher ahead of time.

5. Choose a class hostess. She can assist you in welcoming people, keep in touch with absentees, and clean up afterwards. She can also help monitor your time so that the first or last fifteen minutes can be spent in sharing and prayer.

6. Suggest that each person keep her nametag in her Bible or purse. Encourage the use of the nametags each week for everyone's sake.

7. The sharing time is important for the development of relationships. Be ready with a prayer request or praise if the women are slow to begin. That will encourage others. You may vary the format. Pray conversationally at the end, or have someone pray immediately as each request is given. Be careful of time-hogs. Do not skimp on this time of prayer and sharing. It is essential for the spiritual growth of the group.

8. Members of the Women's Ministries Board will sometimes visit different classes. The board is always available to help. (Here we provide a list of the names and phone numbers of the Women's Ministries Board.)

Elective Class Suggestions

SKILL DEVELOPMENT

Counted Cross Stitch
English Smocking
Knitting
Country Crafts
Quilting
Stenciling
Crocheted Vests
Calligraphy
Flower Arrangements
Collars and Sweats
Needlepoint
Crocheted Heart Rug
Christmas Crafts
Painted House Fire Screen
Cover It with Fabric
Craft Potpourri
Knitted Sweatshirts and
    Fabric Tee Shirts
Needle Knows (basic sewing)
Finishing Touch (women bring their
    own projects to complete here)
Creative Memories
Stock Market 101
Basics of Interior Design
Rubber Stamping

CHRISTIAN LIFE

Scripture Memory
Training in Evangelism/Discipleship
Lay Support Counseling Training
Discipleship as a Lifestyle
Prayer: Key to Spiritual Fitness
Fundamentals of Biblical Counseling
Missions: Out There Somewhere?
How to Study the Bible on Your Own
Behold Your God
Bible Study Follow-up
A Look at 1 Peter
Attributes of God in Exodus
New Age Movement
Pursuing the Power of Prayer
Remedial Quiet Time 101
Living the Reality of What Christ
    Began
One Bold Voice and Two Shaky
    Knees (adult evangelism)
Planting Productive Seed
    (child evangelism)
Praying for Character Qualities in
    One Another
Intercessory Prayer
Finding Your Spiritual Gifts

FAMILY HELPS

Nutrition: Key to a Healthy Family
Tennis
Aerobics
Time Management and
    Home Organization
Hospitality at Your Home

The How-to's of Home Education
Parenting Principles for the Difficult
    Years
Mom-to-Mom
Chinese Cooking
Cake Decorating

FAMILY HELPS (continued)

Search for Significance
CPR
Microwave Cooking
So You're Not Betty Crocker
Beyond Chicken Soup and Castor Oil
The Career of Homemaking
Kidding Around with Kids
Legal Matter Chatter
Good Grief
Home Sweet Home
Do the Most with What You Have
In Search of the Lost Art
  (homemaking)
Forever Lovely
Weight Management
Christian Dating: The Single Dilemma

Things They Never Told You in
  Childbirth Class
Changing Lives Through
  Encouragement
Coping with Codependency
How to Remember to Remember
Responsible Financial Stewardship
Decorative Designs
All About Aging
Parenting Adolescents
Parenting Adult Children
Guiding Your Children's Sexual Values
Disciplining Children
Ministry of Encouragement
Current Issues for Working Women

N i n e

SPONSORING
SPECIAL EVENTS

When we enjoy a special event such as a weekend retreat or special luncheon we are often unaware of the multitude of details involved in its planning. To help you remember and plan for the details needed to present a really organized event on your first try, this section offers practical guidelines for planning special events such as retreats, luncheons, and Saturday Specials. (Information about planning the Heart-to-Heart tea is given in chapter 11.) We also include some suggestions about how to handle the luncheons and suppers that end each session of the Bible study.

Planning a Women's Retreat

I. Plan ahead

    A. At least one year ahead

        1. Visit and reserve the retreat center

        2. Board selects speaker

    B. Four to six months ahead

        1. Select a theme that complements the speaker's topics

        2. Select committee chairmen

            a. Publicity

            b. Registration

            c. Cabin hostesses

   d. Serendipity
   e. Skits/Entertainment
   f. Music
   g. Free time activities

 C. Two months ahead
  1. Contact the speaker, have her send a photograph for publicity, and, if desired, have her prepare questions for small group follow-up discussion
  2. Begin publicity

 D. Four weeks ahead
  1. Begin registration
  2. Prepare an information booklet that includes such items as the schedule, fellowship group questions, a map of the retreat center, Saturday free time activities, an appreciation page, and space for notes
  3. Purchase gifts for the committee chairmen

II. Divide the responsibility: Committee job descriptions

 A. Publicity
  1. Design and make arrangements for flyers, bulletins, and so on
  2. Contact Sunday school classes with announcements
  3. Make and display posters

 B. Registration
  1. Design and distribute forms
  2. Collect money and registrations
  3. Make room assignments following requests on the forms for first and second choices (some dorms may be indicated as "Early" or "Late" for those who prefer either)
  4. Mail a letter to the registrants giving detailed information about the retreat
  5. Have registration set up at camp
  6. Provide packets and nametags
  7. Coordinate with the Minister to Women, or the Board Chairman, to make scholarships available
  8. Give the bottom of the registration form to the person in charge of carpools.

C. Cabin hostesses
   1. Set the mood for the cabin; welcome guests
   2. Be at camp early with table setup
   3. Set up the table for coffee and hot water for tea
   4. Use the table decorations that will come from the serendipity committee
   5. Provide each hostess with two coffeepots and coffee (regular and decaf)
   6. Keep the hostess table neat at all times

D. Serendipity
   1. Provide table arrangements for the dorm hostesses, the dining room, and the speaker's room
   2. Bring pillow surprises and a gift for each woman (mints, bookmark, magnet)
   3. Make the dorm, chapel, and dining room decorations

E. Skits/Entertainment
   1. Coordinate a special welcome for the first session using skits, singing, props, and/or mixers
   2. Plan for Saturday night; possibilities include a talent show, a takeoff of a popular musical, competitive skits

F. Music coordinator
   1. Select a song leader and a pianist
   2. Select people to do special music at each session (solos, duets, instrumentals)
   3. Bring songbooks or overhead transparencies

G. Free time activities
   1. Select people to facilitate/lead four free time activities
   2. Publicize free time activities prior to the retreat
   3. Provide registration for the activities and collect any costs

III. Solicit feedback

A. Create an evaluation form and make copies for the participants

B. Assure that all retreat attendees complete the evaluation form before leaving the retreat

C. Meet with the Retreat Committee to evaluate and celebrate after the retreat

Planning a Special Luncheon

I. **Purpose: To provide an opportunity for women to:**

A. Participate in an all-women's function and to be exposed to the Women's Ministries Program

B. Bring friends and family to be presented with the gospel message

II. **Planning ahead**

A. Six months ahead: Select the speaker (Women's Ministries Board)

B. Three months ahead: Select committee chairmen

C. Two to four months ahead: Select the theme to be used for publicity and throughout the luncheon; contact the speaker and discuss her topic and ask for a photograph for publicity

D. Three or four weeks ahead: Start selling tickets

E. Three weeks ahead: Pass around a sign-up sheet to recruit some help for the kitchen and decorating committees for the day before the luncheon

F. One week ahead: Phone or send postcard reminder to all helpers

G. Day of luncheon: Recognize and thank all committees and helpers; give a small thank-you gift (e.g., Christmas ornament at Christmas)

III. **Committee job descriptions**

A. Publicity and Tickets
   1. Design invitations, tickets, and posters
   2. Make arrangements with the Communications Coordinator for announcements, bulletins, and other churchwide publications
   3. Design and sell tickets

B. Menu
   1. Consider the limitations of hot versus cold menu items; make a decision based on the number of people served
   2. Work with the food service to order and prepare the food or have it catered

C. Decorations
   1. Set up a welcome table including nametags, flowers, and centerpieces
   2. Provide centerpieces for tables
   3. Coordinate decorations for the stage/platform area

D. Music
   1. Select a song leader
   2. Select a piano player
   3. Select someone to do special music
   4. Have taped music or pianist playing while people arrive

Planning a Saturday Special

I. **Purpose: To provide an opportunity for women to:**
   A. Keep in touch during the summer months

   B. Be exposed to the Women's Ministries Program if they have not participated

   C. Bring friends and family to be presented with the gospel message

II. **Responsibilities of the Special Events Coordinator**
   A. Have the board select speakers and dates

   B. Work with the Electives Coordinator to select four diverse electives and appropriate leaders

   C. Have elective leaders give descriptions, costs, and class sizes for the brochure

   D. Determine if participants will bring sack lunches or if the event will be catered

   E. Design the registration brochure and have the Communications Coordinator take care of additional publicity

   F. Start registration three to four weeks in advance

Finishing Well

It is fun to be creative as you plan the end-of-session meal. The daytime program closes with a luncheon; the evening program concludes with a supper.

Sometimes we ask everyone to bring a salad or a dessert. It is helpful to suggest that each elective class be responsible for only two desserts—that way you secure a balance of main dishes and salads. We provide the beverages.

Another thing the women have enjoyed is to buy ingredients for a taco salad. We charge a small amount to cover additional costs (e.g., $3.00 per person). The board and volunteers come the day before to set up and decorate the tables.

When we plan a supper for the evening session, most women prefer a small charge for the meal, and usually several will be willing to bring a dessert. These women especially enjoy the opportunity to eat together in a relaxed atmosphere.

We try to keep variety in our planning and menu, for we know that creates greater anticipation and enjoyment—and having the tables decorated, even very simply, provides a feminine and festive atmosphere.

T e n

REMEMBERING OTHERS THROUGH OUTREACH AND SUPPORT

Many women feel isolated today, as we mentioned previously. Not only do they face the pressures of our declining culture: incest, child abuse, divorce, pornography, but they also experience the same kinds of pressures women have faced historically: the demands of small children, wisdom in discipline, balancing children's needs with husbands' needs, juggling work with home responsibilities and personal need. Women today face all these challenges, frequently without the support of an extended family enjoyed by prior generations. The church today has the privilege of providing that familial role with support and encouragement to women facing such formidable tasks.

This chapter describes the ministries and gives some of the history behind the groups our church formed to meet these varied needs of our women. Appendix 3 gives the instruction sheets we distribute for the various outreach and support ministries.

Abortion Recovery

The purpose of this ministry is to become a Good Samaritan to those who have been hurt by abortion. One of our women conducts an abortion recovery course that helped her after eighteen years of dealing with the guilt of abortion. Through a ten-week Bible study, the women served by this ministry are shown how God sees abortion, and through the group time they learn how to experience God's forgiveness and grace. Some of these women then give their testimonies to encourage others to find healing.

This course has been a blessing and source of healing for the women who have taken it. It goes without saying that this group is strictly confidential and that members' names are not publicly known.

Cancer Support: "Uplifters" and "CanSupport"

One day a woman suggested to me that women like herself who had undergone a mastectomy could support other women as they face that crisis. I was delighted with the idea. We met with several other women in the church with this experience, and they set up goals and guidelines. They named themselves "The Uplifters." They come immediately to the side of any woman facing even a biopsy, and they continue to support those who actually have a mastectomy. Emphasis is placed on a one-to-one relationship where family and personal needs can be met. They serve all the women each year by arranging for the mobile unit from Baylor Medical Center to come to the church campus for mammograms at a reduced rate. The mammography mobile unit is at the church for two days (the same days that the main Women's Ministries sessions are held), and the Uplifters handle the scheduling of appointments.

"CanSupport" was developed out of the Uplifters program and is a support group for those who are suffering from any kind of cancer or who are caring for a cancer patient. The group meets monthly. The group keeps in touch between meetings with phone calls and lunches, thereby maintaining an atmosphere of faith and caring. They provide spiritual and prayer support while ministering to one another in practical ways.

Captain Casserole

This committee was begun to utilize leftover food from our Wednesday night dinners at church. Volunteers prepare supplemental casseroles in disposable containers, which are then stored in the church freezer. This food is available for people who have an illness in the family, for new mothers, or for anyone in our church who needs help with meals.

Care Givers

The ministry of the support groups often surfaces situations in which personal counseling is needed. If a leader feels she is out of her depth, she refers that person to me. If I think it's beyond my range, I refer the woman to professional Christian counselors we trust. But we developed a lay counseling group, called "Care Givers," a core of wise, mature women, each of whom can take a troubled person under her wing and be a friend to her. We offer classes each year to increase their counseling skills. I often refer women to them, or ask one of them to step in and help someone out. They are having a very effective ministry.

Church Office or Library Assistance

These volunteers assist the staff in the church office with special projects or large mailings that require extra hands. Library volunteers sign up for specific times to hold the library open for operation.

Citizens' Awareness Table

This table, available at each Women's Ministries Program session, provides information about local, state, and national issues. Through it, women are encouraged to become involved in the political process by taking action that can make a difference. Such actions include contacting their elected representative by letter, phone, or in person; writing letters to the editors of newspapers; and, especially, being an informed voter.

Crisis Pregnancy Center (CPC)

This Christian ministry is dedicated to assisting women who are experiencing an unplanned pregnancy. It offers practical, constructive alternatives to abortion and helps meet the emotional, practical, and spiritual needs of the mother. We encourage the training of our women to become counselors in Crisis Pregnancy Center offices, to answer abortion hot lines, to baby-sit, or to help this ministry in any way. We also support the CPC in our area with a monthly financial gift.

Divorce Recovery Group

This group provides support and encouragement for women facing the major adjustments that follow a divorce. It may also include women whose adult children are experiencing a divorce, with the complications to family life that this entails.

Evening Bible Study for Business and Professional Women

This Bible study ministers to working women. The group meets at the church to help the women deal with the special problems women encounter in the workplace and to apply scriptural principles to them.

Hand-in-Hand (Widows' Support Group)

This group provides a new widow with assistance in coping with her grief as well as opportunities for fellowship through regular meetings and interesting field trips. The group compiled an information packet for the new widow. When a woman is newly widowed, one of the members of this group is selected to invest personal time and interest in ministering to her during the transition period.

These women have discovered that a monthly Sunday dinner in a restaurant provides a special time of regular fellowship, in addition to other occasional trips and activities.

Homeless Outreach

One year we ministered through the Dallas Life Foundation (a downtown shelter for the homeless) by collecting and delivering used clothing, household goods, toiletries, and personal items. We also furnished Bibles and hymnals, held a weekly women's Bible study and a monthly birthday party, as well as collected grocery receipts to exchange for a computer.

Later, we supported a shelter for battered women and children in several ways: by collecting clothing and household items for their thrift store; by holding a Tuesday morning shower for baby formula, diapers, and other items needed for a newborn; and by implementing an evangelistic birthday party for Jesus.

Currently we are supplying needs (irons, ironing boards, cleaning supplies) for a new homeless shelter. We are also showing the *Jesus* film as an evangelistic outreach and are combining efforts with our Men's Ministry, which is painting the outside of the building.

Hospital Visitation

This group brings spiritual encouragement to women who are ill or have had surgery. Hospital or home visits are also made to women who have close family members in the hospital. Depending upon the individual situation, the committee members send cards, make telephone calls, and take food to the homes of the women served by this ministry.

Infertility

This is a group of women suffering from infertility. The group meets monthly to encourage each other with prayer, support, and information, and to celebrate adoptions or births.

Marriage Enrichment

We frequently hold electives in marriage enrichment. This ministry of encouragement often continues to meet on its own. The Women's Ministries Program provides an umbrella under which all of these marriage enrichment groups function. That structure gives them security, status, and accountability.

Mom-to-Mom

An elective called "Mom-to-Mom" became an adjunct ministry after a group of young mothers did not want to end the mutual support when the elective concluded. The group meets once a month during the school year, invites appropriate speakers, has a picnic for moms and their kids in June, maintains a prayer chain, and helps decorate the church nursery by painting bright murals. Experienced moms in our church are also invited to meet with them to share their wisdom. Many other groups have found that M.O.P.S., a program for mothers of preschoolers, can become an effective portion of their Women's Ministries Program.

Newcomers

The Welcoming Newcomers Committee receives the visitors' cards from the church office and phones the visiting women. They welcome them to the church and inform them about the Women's Ministries Program as well as answer any questions they may have about other church activities.

New Mothers

This committee ministers to women in our church body who have recently welcomed new babies into their homes, either by birth or by adoption. Our purpose is to show support and encouragement by a personal visit either at the hospital or at home. We have taken such little gifts as the Golden Book *Prayers for Children* or a calligraphy print of Psalm 127:3. This year we are giving the new mothers a packet of verses that relate to mothering and child rearing to encourage memorization.

Nursing Homes

This outreach obtains the names of those from our church in nursing homes and visits them. They take small remembrances, such as flowers, cards, or cookies. Other times the women have presented special music, given a devotional, or led a Bible Study.

Sharing Closet

The purpose of this closet is to meet the needs of our missionaries who are home on furlough, members of our church, and other needy people. Examples of items collected are gently worn clothing, household items, and, if you have the room, furniture in good repair.

Special Missions Projects

Taping our weekly Bible lessons continues to be a popular missions project. We send them worldwide to our women missionaries. Other projects have included

- Making individual prayer cards for missionaries
- Sewing mosquito nets for missionaries in Africa
- Making wordless books and bean bags for child evangelism clubs
- Providing financial support for short-term missionaries
- Donating clothing and money for Bibles for Romania
- Giving money for materials for our men's and high school ministries to build homes for widows in Guatemala
- Financial support for a sister church in Austria that provides Bibles and starter kits for homemaking for refugee families

Special Needs Children

A parent who has a child with special needs volunteered to organize a Sunday school class for children of all ages who might not benefit from regular classes.

Twelve-Step Study Group

This group meets once a week to encourage and support one another in changing codependent behaviors into emotionally healthy lifestyles in order to serve the Lord more effectively. We use *The Twelve Steps: A Spiritual Journey* (San Diego: Recovery) as our guide.

Tutoring Ministry

Some of our women tutor in a program that provides personal encouragement as well as academic tutoring in an inner-city school. This program is offered as an elective in the weekly program. Volunteers carpool to the school and meet with students on a one-on-one basis. The women pray together for their students immediately after the students return to class. The program continues even when the Women's Ministries Program is not in session. The elective provides the students with role models for character development and encouragement to pursue further educational opportunities.

Eleven

A SPECIAL GARDEN:
HEART-TO-HEART

A most successful program we call "Heart-to-Heart" in our church assists in developing the important and supportive friendships between older women, "Seniors," and younger women, "Juniors." Because women uniquely understand women, have gone through similar experiences, and feel the same emotions, they can provide sympathetic listening and godly counsel and often defuse tense personal situations before they escalate into major crises.

Spiritually mature women provide a biblical perspective of life, with their sound working knowledge of the Scriptures and a solid track record of godly choices and conduct.

The experience, empathy, maturity, and spirituality of these women represent an enormously powerful reservoir of untapped, God-given resource from which the church can greatly benefit. Women need it; Scripture commands it. The Heart-to-Heart program taps this reservoir.

Because it is flexible, the Heart-to-Heart program can be initiated in any way that suits your church, consistent with its size and culture. Informal gatherings, such as coffees or brunches, can be used to kick off the program, enabling women to meet each other and quickly establish areas of common interest. The general women's meetings, Sunday school classes and worship services can be used for recruiting participants. We provide each woman with a profile sheet to facilitate the matching process (see Appendix 6). For better success in matching, we attempt to pair women holding at least two interests or life issues in common.

Here are some guidelines we have found effective for the development of meaningful relationships.

- Make a one-year commitment to the relationship
- Contact each other once a week and meet at least once a month
- Pray for each other regularly
- Do things together (whether it be Bible study, shopping, learning a new skill, or just going to lunch; each set of partners is free to do what they want as long as they work on developing the relationship)

What Does It Look Like?

This ministry works. Some older women enjoy it so much that they meet with several younger women. Younger women love these friendships. They feel loved and have someone to call on for support and wisdom. As mentioned earlier, the isolation and loneliness women feel is not so much that communication between men and women has broken down, but rather that in our fast-paced society communication between women and women has broken down. Women need other women. Heart-to-Heart provides a vehicle to facilitate that contact.

This ministry serves primarily as a source of encouragement. It is not necessarily a formal discipleship program, nor an in-depth counseling service, but rather it is meaningful friendship for support, guidance, love, and encouragement. In addition, we ask the partners to pray with each other, for by prayer we truly begin to understand the heart of the other woman and we experience the presence of God in our developing relationships.

Approximately 50 percent of our young women came from broken homes; therefore, they seek role models from women who can provide hope and confidence that lifelong marriage is a realistic possibility. Others want encouragement and advice on how to live with purity and integrity in their single and/or professional lives. Many have come to know the Lord but were not reared in godly homes; thus they don't know what it looks like to be a woman who lives to please God.

We also have women who move into our city and miss their former support system of older women. One twenty-five-year-old woman related how much she not only missed her mom but her mom's friends and her friends' moms. She described her observations and thoughts after attending our Women's Ministries Program like this: "These are such women-women, and I am such a girl-woman! How will I ever attain the maturity I have seen in them?"

As you might anticipate, she was the first to sign up for Heart-to-Heart that year, and her new friendships provided special blessings.

Of course, we have mature and immature young women who simply enjoy the company and friendship of an older woman who shares a godly perspective and who has lived a little longer. In fact, life experience represents the primary credentials we stress to our older, senior women. We emphasize the opportunity God gives them to invest what He has taught them throughout their lives into the lives of younger women. Experiences of joyful times as well as trials and heartaches where they discovered God real and sufficient represent the resources they offer another woman. Their practical knowledge gleaned from life experiences provides perspective and wisdom for a younger woman. Many have God-given nurturing qualities that have been wonderfully developed.

In the comfort of this nurturing relationship with an older woman, many young women find it easier or safer to share their fears and insecurities than with their peers. Furthermore, older women have a unique ability to comfort and encourage which younger women find to be special.

Win Couchman describes a mentoring relationship in this way.

> On Christmas Eve, a deep San Francisco-style fog kept our car crawling blindly along the road. Suddenly another car pulled onto the road right ahead of us. Because we were now following a set of beautiful twin taillights, we could safely increase our speed from fifteen to twenty-five miles per hour. A mentor is someone farther on down the road from you, who is going where you want to go, and who is willing to give you some light to help you get there![1]

Older women have much to share. They become true friends to the younger women. Yet, happily, this relationship is a two-way street. The younger woman ministers to and cares for the older woman as well. The focus is to encourage one another to depend upon God, not upon the relationship. Therefore, the Bible, not just personal experiences, forms the standard and authority in the relationship.

The Heart-to-Heart program is simple to begin in a church of any size. Your older women may need your encouragement to accept the role of seniors, because generally they do not recognize the true value of their maturity and life experience. That life experience is their credential for this relationship. The Heart-to-Heart program becomes a source of healing, strength, and growth as the spiritually mature women give meaningful influence in the lives of other women.

As women's unique needs are met by these godly role models, the families, the church, and the community will be blessed.

How to Start

ADMINISTRATION

The Heart-to-Heart Coordinator serves on the Women's Ministries Board, and her primary function is to oversee the operation of the Heart-to-Heart ministry of Senior and Junior partners. Her responsibilities are listed in the job descriptions of the Women's Ministries Board in chapter 7.

Rather than the terms *Senior* and *Junior,* some churches use *Naomi* and *Ruth* and others use *Elizabeth* and *Mary.* Needed forms, guidelines, and examples to assist you in developing your own program are found in Appendix 6.

The coordinator needs the help of an assistant with whom to brainstorm and speak confidentially. These two women need to share in prayer and seek each other's wisdom, especially when making matches. They use their knowledge of their women as well as the completed profile sheets to make the matches. If possible they should match women who share at least two interests or life situations in common, more if possible.

There should be an appropriate age span between the partners. Generally, women under thirty-five are Juniors, women between thirty-five and forty-five are either, and women forty-five and over are Seniors. Some women in their late twenties and thirties can become a Senior to a very young woman, and can also become a Junior to an older woman. Just be careful not to be too rigid about age guidelines. One year, for example, we had a twenty-one-year-old—who was still in college and had been married only two months—sign up. We were able to match her with a twenty-nine year old who had been married eight years, had a seven-year-old daughter, and who in terms of experience and spiritual maturity was able to minister to her new, younger friend. On the other hand, we matched a fifty-one-year-old woman, who was a new believer and who had just been married for the first time, with a godly seventy-year-old widow who had enjoyed a long and wonderful marriage.

The more you study the profiles of the interests, ages, personalities, and spiritual maturity of your women, the more effective your matches will be. Most important of all, *pray!* We never make a match unless we have peace about it. We have seen the Lord put women together for reasons that we could never have anticipated.

Once the match is made, the Senior partner initiates the first call to her Junior. After that, however, calling should be reciprocal.

THE STEERING COMMITTEE

Together the coordinator and her assistant develop a steering committee to assist in following up with the matched partners during the year to keep the program functioning well. The steering committee consists of trustworthy Junior and Senior women serving two-year terms. They each receive a list of matches. They are responsible to pray for those women and call them regularly. Juniors and Seniors are contacted alternately throughout the year; therefore, each woman is contacted bimonthly to assure that she and her partner are meeting and to affirm that the relationship is progressing well. The steering committee woman records the partner's general comments in her card file.

We must be careful not to offend by treating women as though the partners are children, and we must use common sense. When calling, for example, it is helpful to have some information to convey, such as an upcoming church luncheon or tea that would be fun to attend with her partner. If you have seen the woman and she tells you about her relationship, there is no need to contact her again. But, in general, plan on calling the women on alternate months. Your calling provides key accountability for a successful Heart-to-Heart program, and it also helps your women feel special, cared for, and part of a larger whole of committed and growing women.

This ongoing contact allows small problems to be identified quickly and to enhance the effectiveness of the program. As I have spoken with those who have experienced difficulties in their Heart-to-Heart program, most often they have omitted this crucial element of oversight, and difficulties are not resolved quickly.

REFER SERIOUS PROBLEMS

Other more serious problems will be surfaced in these regular calls. At that point the committee member needs to discuss them with the Heart-to-Heart coordinator. She will know how to proceed from there. If the problem proves severe, the coordinator should seek help from her authority within the Women's Ministry program.

The most common difficulty is that of overcommitment. Often, when a match is not working well, inquiry by the committee person will find one of the partners is too busy. The committee person can give the partner a graceful out and remake the match.

The coordinator and assistant coordinator should call their steering committee members monthly to gain feedback on how the matches are progressing. The coordinator keeps a file of the profile sheets, brochures, and suggestions.

Heart-to-Heart Record Card

Here is an example of the follow-up record card used by our steering committee. As we mentioned, this follow-up supports the success of the program. It helps to jot down the comments and adjustments made to continually improve the way you are making matches.

HEART-TO-HEART RECORD CARD
(For the committee to keep in touch with participants)

Name _____

Address _____ Jr. _____ Sr._____

City _____ Zip _____

Home phone _____ Work phone _____

Age _____ Married _____ Single _____

Partner assigned _____

Dates called   Comments

_____   _____

_____   _____

_____   _____

_____   _____

Steering Committee Member assigned: _____

Helpful to use on a 5 x 8 card
These should be color-coded for Junior and Senior Partners

Timing for Sign-ups

We have found September or October to be the optimum time for sign-ups for Heart-to-Heart, but certainly choose a month most convenient to your own situation. Women's lives, especially those with school-age children, tend to operate on a school calendar. Plan to publicize and allow sign-ups for an entire month.

As much as possible try to limit making matches to within that sign-up time, rather than trying as we did at first, to match people all year long. You can make exceptions, but it complicates the program as it grows.

After completing the matches, hold a special event that will be enjoyable. That gathering will give each match a head start. Partners can be called and notified of the match prior to the event, or part of the event can consist of matching the pairs in creative ways. This event also provides an opportunity for giving suggestions for activities for the partners. At the end of this chapter are some training guidelines used one year at our opening event.

At Northwest Bible Church we have a kickoff dinner in October. The matches have already been made and the pairs meet for the first time. After the meal, there is a training session for the Seniors and the Juniors separately. The speakers give general guidelines for the relationship with suggestions for activities. Other churches have used an event such as a picnic to introduce the pairs.

In the spring we host a Heart-to-Heart tea. We have been delighted to discover the benefits of giving this tea. First, it provides another way for us to say "We love you" to our women through serving them. Second, it makes our women feel special and feminine, and it teaches them hospitality. Finally, it gives our women a nonthreatening event to invite friends who do not know Christ personally.

Some churches use an evening meal rather than a tea to acquaint the women with the program. During the program a speaker gives the scriptural and practical reasons for the mentor relationship. Profile sheets are ready for the women to use in signing up.

The fall kickoff event, the spring Heart-to-Heart tea, and even a special event at the end of the year give the mentor partners the sense that they are part of something bigger than just the two of them!

Fall Kickoff Event

PUBLICITY

1. Spend the month of September advertising
   a. Make announcements and provide information and sign-up tables throughout the church
   b. Place announcements in the church bulletins and newsletters
2. Host a sign-up coffee (or coffees) or a dinner
   a. Give one on a Saturday to accommodate women working outside the home
   b Provide nametags, profile sheets, and Heart-to-Heart brochures
   c. The coordinator or her assistant initiates a time of group sharing, during which the concept and commitment of Heart-to-Heart is presented; the coordinator should also encourage group interaction by presenting two or three self-revealing questions from which each chooses one to share with the group
   d. Ascertain if any women present wish to be matched together
3. Pass the word along! Encourage partners to tell others how wonderful the program is and how God has used it to minister to them

The Heart-to-Heart Tea

The annual afternoon spring tea is an effective way to attract new Seniors and Juniors to the program. We schedule the tea for the first Friday of March at 2:00 P.M. and call it "Tea at Two." This is a lovely opportunity to enjoy the fellowship of women of all ages and to hear testimonies about the joy of the Heart-to-Heart relationship.

The timing allows women several months to consider what they have just heard and be better prepared to make a commitment in the next fall sign-up.

This event is arranged by the Heart-to-Heart committee, but it's promoted through the Women's Ministries Program and to the whole church, because it is a key means for recruiting participants. We invite all women who regularly attend our church. Reservations are necessary for proper planning. We also provide a nursery for children kindergarten age and younger.

This tea accomplishes several goals. First, it helps to publicize the Heart-to-Heart ministry in an unpressured atmosphere. We offer material, have a Senior share her testimony, and provide an occasion where younger and older women are together enjoying each other's company. This is not a sign-up time! However, we find that many Seniors join the following fall after having had the summer months to think over all they heard and experienced at the tea.

Second, the tea provides a delightful atmosphere for partners to enjoy each other's company. It also gives the committee a special opportunity to serve our women lovingly and graciously. When the women come, they feel part of a ministry that cares deeply about them. Furthermore, there is something wonderful about going to an event that is lovely and completely feminine. Our hope is that this time of fellowship and spiritual encouragement will enhance the joy of being a Christian woman.

During the tea we always have a guest speaker share her testimony, give a book review, or relate an experience of great spiritual growth and dependence upon God. There are certainly other topics of interest that could be covered. We are simply careful not to duplicate the style of our weekly Bible study. Our women have been deeply touched by these Heart-to-Heart teas, and several guests have trusted Christ as Savior.

Our women love the Heart-to-Heart tea and look forward to it each year. Yes, it does require time and detailed planning, but it is also fun! Be creative, read books on formal and informal teas, and involve your women. We were surprised to realize we were teaching many young women hospitality skills. We were also happy to see what a bonding experience working on such a project can be among women. Most of all, keep an attitude of loving service during all of your preparations and pray that all will be done for God's glory.

The next few pages contain some detailed planning sheets used by one of our Heart-to-Heart coordinators who was very creative and gifted in detail; she even developed a minute-by-minute plan for the program. As you will see, she got great joy from serving in this position. You may glean some ideas from her enthusiasm. However, you certainly do not have to be so elaborate.

ROOM PREPARATIONS AND TABLE SETTINGS

Round tables for guests
Tables for coffee, tea, and food
White tablecloths
Podium
Piano
Table for nametags and informational materials
Taping and sound system
Floral arrangements or centerpieces
Two silver services
Two extra coffeepots for quick replenishing
Two crystal or silver water pitchers
Four white linen cloths for holding under pitchers
Extra silver trays for food
Several candelabra and long white candles
China cups and plates
Doilies, white and lacy
Water glasses
Spoons, forks
Napkins, folded
Two spoons or tongs for sugar
Crystal or china dish for lemon slices
Crystal bowl for mints
(Many of these items can be rented, if necessary)

COMMITTEE RESPONSIBILITIES

Food planning
Name tags
Heart-to-Heart information
Flowers
Pianist
Senior testimony and speaker
Tea server
Coffee server
Greeters
Replenish tea and coffee
Replenish food

Bulletin announcements
Group reminders or invitations
    Letter invitations to the matched partners
    Nursery arrangements
    Sunday school announcements
    Honorarium or gift for the speaker and the pianist
    Secure cleanup committee

FOOD SUGGESTIONS

Coffee, Tea, and Treats
    Gourmet coffee (e.g., Vanilla Praline)
    Gourmet tea (e.g., Passion Blend or fruit)
    Iced water with lemon slices and mint leaves
    Lemon slices (stuck with cloves in middle) for tea table
    Cream, really *milk,* for tea and coffee
    Sugar, lump or granulated, for tea and coffee
    Buttered mints on tea and coffee tables

Food Ideas
Portions are small, dainty morsels
    Tea sandwiches—crusts always removed
        slivered ham
        slice of cucumber or watercress with herbed butter
        cream cheese with date nut bread
    Lemon pound cake
    Pear or apple cake
    Pumpkin nut bread or muffins
    Lemon thyme bread
    Milk and honey bread with honey butter
    Hot mini-muffins
    Sponge cake with a layer of strawberry jam and whipped cream
    Cream cakes
    Small cheesecakes with raspberries or kiwi on top
    Fruitcake squares
    Scones with preserves and whipped cream
    Shortbreads
    Crumpets
    Cookies, wafers

Petite madeleines
Lemon squares
Petits fours
Fancy pastries
Jam tarts
Chocolate-covered strawberries or dried apricots
Fresh fruit

SCHEDULE

10:30 Begin setting up, folding napkins, etc.
       Food can be delivered until 1:30
       Pray together
1:30   Instruct servers
       Check room
1:45   Bring out food and drinks
1:50   Be ready! Piano playing, ready to greet and serve for the early birds
2:00   1. Greet, give nametags, offer Heart-to-Heart book
       2. Guide to food tables, plates with doilies
       3. Guide to coffee (always on the side of the table closest to the entrance) or tea (always on the side of the table farthest from the entrance); spoons on drink tables
       4. Guests find table and friends; each table has folded beautiful napkins, forks, and a floral centerpiece
2:35   Announce that guests have two more minutes before the program begins
2:37   Welcome warmly (chairman)
       Introduce Senior
2:39   Senior testimony
2:42   Introduce speaker
2:43   Speaker begins
3:15   Speaker finishes
3:16   Chairman thanks the speaker and guests for coming; she invites the guests to return for more refreshments
3:30   Nursery closes, tea officially ends
3:50   Tea really ends; clean up
4:30   Go home and collapse!

Common Questions for
Problem Solving as Matches Are Made

QUESTION:
What if there are not enough older women in your church?

ANSWER:
Until your church attracts more older women or until your women grow old, ask your spiritually mature women in their thirties to serve as Seniors. Then inform your unmatched Juniors that you will match them as soon as a Senior is available.

Also, plan to ask Seniors to take on more than one Junior. This works well. Some of our older women have as many as six Heart-to-Heart partners. However, it is important that you not give more than one Senior to a Junior.

In addition, only match women who regularly attend your church. You are not responsible to provide Seniors for young women visiting your Women's Ministries Program from other churches.

QUESTION:
What if there are a greater number of older women than younger?

ANSWER:
Rejoice! Begin your program. The younger women of your church and community will be drawn like magnets to your older women. Emphasize the aspect of friendship to your younger women. Some churches have told us that their younger women were hesitant to respond because they mistakenly believed this to be an authoritative relationship.

QUESTION:
What if only a handful of women are truly excited about this ministry?

ANSWER:
Then start with a handful! As these relationships grow and develop, the joy and satisfaction will be gradually contagious. Continue to teach about the importance of intergenerational friendship.

QUESTION:
How do we encourage our older women to respond? They seem fearful or insecure about their ability to minister to a younger woman.

ANSWER:
First, ask Seniors in the program to call their friends in your church who are spiritually mature to tell them about the ministry and the need. Second, have Seniors publicly share about their experiences with younger women. Some older women feel

intimidated because they think they must be an expert Bible teacher, intellectual genius, or spiritual giant to fill this role. But when they hear other women share, they can relate and realize how very much they too have to offer. Emphasize the life experience and friendship aspects of the relationship. Remind them of the value of their life experience.

QUESTION:

What if a Senior signs up who is spiritually immature or emotionally needy? She would simply not be an appropriate role model.

ANSWER:

First, pray and be kind, loving, and sensitive to her needs. Talk to her and ask her why she is interested in this program. Many times women will admit they would rather be a Junior, but because of their age, they signed up to be a Senior. Invite them to be Juniors. If this alternative doesn't arise, keep talking. You might find they are extremely busy. Suggest that they wait to avoid overcommitment; they can still minister to younger women through Bible study and church. If they are skilled in another area (choir, administrative) suggest they are truly more needed in that area at present. Ask God to help you find a kind and appropriate reason to suggest their not becoming a Senior. If none of these suggestions works, you may be in a situation where you have to say lovingly, "I think you are dealing with so much in your own life at this time that I believe it would be better to wait. In the meantime, how can we be of help to you?" Or, you might tell her that because she is such a new Christian, you believe it would be best for her to wait a couple of years before becoming a Senior. Then suggest other areas of ministry in which she could serve.

QUESTION:

What if an extremely needy Junior signs up?

ANSWER:

Again, pray first and then talk with her. Explain that she needs an older woman's influence and example in her life. But also explain that Heart-to-Heart is not structured to meet the kind of time demand and/or the kind of counseling she needs to receive. Tell her you would like to help her find a ministry that would better meet her needs. Lay counseling or professional help might be appropriate. You may find you have an older woman who considers her ministry helping those with deep troubles. Ask your leadership for help if you cannot find an alternative. We have a group of lay women whose skills have been sharpened through courses we offer in our electives. They are available to offer strong, wise support to women who need counsel to change their lifestyle and attitudes and actions, or who live in difficult, ongoing situations. Perhaps your pastor would work with you in developing a group such as this in your church.

QUESTION:

How do we avoid problems of gossip?

ANSWER:

Place continual emphasis on the teaching of Titus 2, not to be malicious gossips. Choose Seniors who have a reputation of confidentiality. Emphasize the responsibility and privilege of confidentiality when you speak with Juniors and Seniors at various meetings.

QUESTION:

How do we make sure these relationships are strong, close, and growing?

ANSWER:

You can't. However, you can encourage, pray for, and remind the women to keep the relationships close and growing Moreover, the structure of calls and availability of committee women for input and encouragement does bring a level of accountability. But the relationship is in the hands of the Lord and of the Junior and Senior women who have made their commitments to each other. They are the ones truly responsible for their relationship.

Though some matches may not "take" in spite of your best efforts, do not be discouraged. The vast majority will prove to be a great blessing and well worth the energy you put into this work.

Suggested Questions for Getting Acquainted

- Tell me about your family
  (husband, children, etc.)
- Tell me about your activities
  (work, leisure, etc.)
- Tell me one interesting or unique thing about you
- Tell me about your Heart-to-Heart experiences
  (involvement, reason for signing up, etc.)
- Tell me one thing you would like to accomplish this year through Heart-to-Heart

Preparing to Meet

- Set a time to meet
- Make a list of your goals (in writing)
- Pray for your partner and ask God to open your hearts to one another
- Pray that the Holy Spirit would direct your relationship and that together you would glorify the Father

Goal Setting, Committing, and Praying

• Decide when and how often to get together
• Mutually commit to this schedule, valuing its importance
• Discuss your goals with one another
• Decide on the kind of study or activity you want to share
• Commit to pray for each other and your relationship regularly
• Choose the times to call each other and pray over the phone

Some Activities Others Have Enjoyed That You Can Try

• Do a Bible study
• Memorize a verse together
• Sew a quilt
• Go for a walk
• Attend a craft show
• Meet for pie and coffee
• Attend an event at church together
• Share a sack lunch
• Share your trials and triumphs
• Go to a play together
• Share your favorite recipes
• Go shopping
• Meet for yogurt

> LOVE IS NOT A RESERVOIR THAT CAN RUN DRY.
> IT IS A NATURAL SPRING—
> THE LONGER AND FURTHER IT FLOWS,
> THE STRONGER AND DEEPER IT BECOMES.

Recent Profile Sheet Comments

Here are some comments from profile sheets completed by the Seniors in answer to the question, *What I am looking for in Heart-to-Heart?*

• "Friendship and a chance to give back."

141

- "I'd like to find a younger woman to build a friendship with, to love and encourage to walk closely with the Lord, pray with, and have fun with."
- "An opportunity to share my experiences (mistakes), strengths, and hopes with someone who wants it."
- "Someone to be a big sister to and share my life with."
- "Would love to meet someone's needs by sharing how faithful God has been in meeting all my needs in the business world and with three children and a husband."
- "Sharing and accountability."
- "Someone who needs or wants a friend who doesn't feel fifty."

Below are some comments by Juniors in response to the same question.

- "An older friend who can encourage me, who has been there and can give me wisdom in some frustrating times when I feel life is out of control."
- "A Christian friend who knows what it feels like to be a mom at home."
- "Someone I can go to for ideas and hints about family life."
- "An older, more mature perspective on running a home and raising a family."
- "After moving seven times in fifteen years I need someone to share with. My mother died when I was twenty-one, so I treasure relationships with older women."
- "Someone to confide in."
- "Someone who can give me honest, mature, biblical insight and feedback."
- "Seeing life from a different perspective—talking to someone who has experienced things I am currently experiencing."
- "My mother lives a long way away, and I would like some nurturing, wisdom, and love by an older woman."
- "I have no relatives in this area and I often get homesick for my mother's company."

Feedback from the Program

Here is some feedback from both Senior and Junior partners who have already participated in Heart-to-Heart.

FROM THE SENIORS

"During these days of 'Hi' and 'Bye' it's easy to have many acquaintances, but not so easy to develop friendships. Heart-to-Heart has given me the *challenge* to really get to know, enjoy, and love some of the younger women in my church; some I probably would never have known."

"As an older woman, I have experienced joyful and not so joyful times as a wife, mother, and homemaker. I am able to encourage younger women in these areas from a Christian perspective. However, I gain as well as give. I enjoy the concern and love I've received, and love their youthful vitality, humor, and enthusiasm for life. It keeps me thinking younger."

"I see my Heart-to-Heart role mainly as an encourager. My junior partners are so bright and capable! I just try to help them see their own abilities and worth."

"I love opportunities to share because I always come out knowing more than when I began. The Lord seems to reveal truth in the midst of Heart-to-Heart sharing. Jesus' command to love one another is uppermost in my walk, and I am hungry to form new relationships that go below the surface. I've learned that giving and receiving are never one-sided and that I need the Body. I look forward to being kept up-to-date by a younger person so I don't get out of touch."

"I want to be of help and encouragement to a young mother, to lend a listening and sympathetic ear, to share my experiences that might apply to her situation. I want to show her how God has been faithful and led me through every trial and met every need of my life."

FROM THE JUNIORS

"I love talking to my senior! She is always nonjudgmental and gives a calm balance to my life. Her strong faith, evident in every situation, is an encouragement. She is a great role model."

"By watching my senior partner demonstrate strength in the midst of tragedy, I learned great lessons about what it means to trust in God, to rest in God, and to know God."

"I have been exceedingly blessed by the spiritual nurturing I have received from my senior partners. One has taught me how to be joyful regardless of circumstances. Another has modeled unselfish giving. My present partner has encouraged me beyond measure to keep time with my Lord and family at the forefront of my life. I so wish to be a godly woman, and I am grateful for their guidance, availability, and loving care."

The Ten Commandments of Mentoring

RELATIONSHIP

The stronger the bonding the more satisfying and fulfilling the friendship. This takes time, understanding, and lots of prayer. Good friendships last forever.

PURPOSE

To help avoid disappointment, aims and expectations should be clearly expressed, negotiated, and agreed upon at the beginning of the mentoring relationship. It is helpful to have this in writing.

REGULARITY

It is helpful to talk this over up front and to set some ground rules both for regular meeting times and for impromptu "get-togethers." Be sensitive to time constraints. Once-a-week contact, face-to-face or by telephone, usually works best.

ACCOUNTABILITY

Mutual responsibility is an important mentoring dynamic, and you must plan for it. Agree together on how you will establish, monitor, and evaluate your growth process.

COMMUNICATION

Special concerns or needs may surface in the course of building the friendship. Timing and procedure for resolving the challenges must be handled with mutual kindness, maturity, and respect. Honesty and openness are vital. Remember that your relationship is to be a warm and loving friendship, not a counseling service.

CONFIDENTIALITY

As the mentoring relationship deepens, sharing of personal matters increases. It is important to honor each partner's personality, feelings, and level of confidentiality. A simple statement to each other requesting conversations be kept private can save much grief at a later date.

MENTORING LIFE CYCLES TIME FRAME

The Northwest Bible Church "Heart-to-Heart" mentoring ministry has *a one-year commitment* for each mentoring pair. Official assignments of new pairs will begin in September and end in May, although the expectation is that the bond of friendships already established will continue within the fellowship of believers.

EVALUATION

From time to time the mentoring relationship should be evaluated for the purpose of redefinition or modification of expectations. Assessment of progress or problems is the primary purpose of the steering committee, whose goal is to assist and nurture each pair in the mentoring relationship.

EXPECTATIONS

Expectations should be realistic in order that dissatisfaction in mentoring not hamper the bonding. Real life situations have complexities, so feedback to one another will encourage down-to-earth hopes and goals.

CLOSURE

Closure has to do with bringing a satisfactory end to a mentoring experience. What frequently happens in successful closure is an ongoing friendship that allows for occasional mentoring and future interweaving of lives. This is one of the most important of the ten commandments of mentoring.

Courtesy Northwest Bible Church, Dallas, Texas

HEART TO HEART

Is anyone there
Who would like to share
in my life as a mother and a wife?
Heart to Heart . . .

Could we pray
or talk through my day
share in my joy and sorrow
today and tomorrow?
Heart to Heart . . .

Would you give me your view
on what I should do
or lend me your ear
to hear my thought so dear?
Heart to Heart . . .

Oh, how I want to live for Jesus
and teach my family how He frees us.
Please show me how to walk in His way
So my life will be full of Him every day
Heart to Heart . . .
            —*Reeve Pearce*

Note

1. Win Couchman, "Cross-Generational Relationships," lecture to Women for Christ, 1983 Winter Brea (tape available from Domain Communications, Wheaton, Illinois, 60187).

Part Four

CULTIVATING
THE GARDEN

The LORD God . . . planted a garden.
GENESIS 2:8

Twelve

TRAINING AND
LEADERSHIP DEVELOPMENT

Until fairly recently feminine leadership in the church was considered by many to be an oxymoron. Women were not supposed to be leaders, just followers supporting leaders. Of course, this presented a problem for women to whom the spiritual gifts of leading, administration, and teaching were given. Did the Holy Spirit make a mistake? Were they given these gifts to frustrate them because there was no place for them to serve? (1 Corinthians 12:11). All these spiritual gifts are the work of one and the same Spirit, and He gives them to each one, just as He determines: "Now to each one the manifestation of the Spirit is given for the common good" (1 Corinthians 12:7). The church has not historically given gifted women a significant place to serve with all the gifts for the edification of the whole body. Yet as we have seen already, God has assigned at least one ministry to women that only women can do (besides being a wife and mother), and that ministry is investing in the lives of other women.

Surely this provides a place for their gifts, creativity, and relational skills to have complete freedom to develop and be a blessing to others. Titus 2:3–5 is clear that spiritually mature women are to teach and train the generations following them, and they are also to be role models of godly womanhood. It's obvious, isn't it, that only a woman can both teach and role model what it looks like for a woman to live to please God? That's something men cannot do. So our ministry is vital. I'm not implying that this is the only area where women can exercise their leadership ability in the local church; there are many things we can do. But this unique area is our baby! No one can do it but us!

The Need Recognized

Today as more churches are recognizing the need to have biblical women's ministries relevant to the needs of today's women, the issue of developing leadership in women becomes critical.

What does feminine leadership look like? Does it mean that women become like men in the way they lead? Does it mean that we take a strident, militant, feminist posture? Does it mean that we go around with a permanent chip on our shoulders? Does it mean that we put aside our natural feminine qualities—our nurturing capabilities and our relational skills in order to be good leaders? The answer is an emphatic NO! Rather, we should bring to leadership those very qualities that define womanhood and bring all the advantages that our gender offers to the leadership of women. The feminine face of leadership will be as distinctive as the difference between men and women.

Jesus the Leadership Model

The comprehensive image of God is the male and female together. Each of us is personally created in God's image, yet there are distinctive differences in the way that image is reflected in the male and female so that we complement and complete each other. That distinctiveness should be evident in the way we lead. We women have a unique contribution to make to everything we touch. Whatever our role, we should want to realize the potential God has for us as *women*. The only man whose leadership style we should follow is our Lord Jesus Christ. We want to be the kind of leader Jesus was.

As always, Jesus is our best model in any area of life. We will be considering a number of aspects of leadership development involved in women's ministry following His example. Jesus *observed, recruited, developed,* and *supported* those He called to follow Him. Let's consider together how we can bring those same aspects of leadership development to bear in the lives of the women we lead in Women's Ministries.

Selecting Leaders

OBSERVATION

Getting people involved in various areas of service gives us the chance to observe their talents and gifts. We can see how well they work as a team member, respecting what the other person has to do and say and cooperating with them. Do they get their job done on time? Do they procrastinate? Are they wise in how they use their time?

Do they volunteer for more than they have time to really do well? Do they always seek recognition and prominence? Are they punctual or always rushing in ten minutes late?

I remember a woman who had many qualifications for leadership except for the fact that she was chronically about forty-five minutes late for everything she had to do, not just in regard to church. This was something she never chose to deal with; thus it disqualified her from serving with us as well.

What do you observe that a person does well and does not do well? Sometimes a very creative person will get so bogged down in details that she fails to communicate the total picture well. Therefore, people become frustrated as they try to help her. In that case, help her see that she will need someone to come alongside to assist her in communication and organization, and to help her clarify what she needs to accomplish. In a good team, each member makes a significant contribution to the whole.

RECRUITING

I am often asked how we select members for the Women's Ministries Board. We do not hold elections. Women are invited to serve. Since each board member is committed to a two-year term, we stagger their terms so only half go off the board each May. We start as early as January to discuss potential candidates for these positions. However, we are always looking for women to develop as leaders who have shown commitment to the Women's Ministries Program.

Here are some of our considerations.

Women who:

- Attend regularly
- May have taught electives
- Often volunteer to serve
- Demonstrate responsibility and skill in service
- Show a love for God in all they do
- Love and care for other women
- Are members of our church

We also look at their giftedness. For instance, when we look for an outreach coordinator, we want someone who can organize, delegate, and supervise the various ministries under her care. When we want a hospitality coordinator, we look for a woman who is warm, creative, and hospitable in her own home. When the board agrees unanimously to invite a woman to fill a position, I call or visit personally with her.

APPROACH

After encouraging her about my observations of her interest and enthusiastic support of Women's Ministries, I ask her several questions, such as those below and give appropriate explanations and encouragement:

- *Are you a member of the church?*
  If the answer is no, are you willing to become a member of the church?

  If she is not, everything else I will say is dependent upon her being willing to join. (We do not require church membership for participation in Women's Ministries Programs, but we do require it for a board position.)

- *How involved are you this coming year in other activities?*

  If she has many commitments, I ask if any are ending soon. If none are, I suggest waiting for another year. If some are ending, I continue and explain the position that is open, describing some of its responsibilities.

- *Does this position suit your interests and your gifts?*

  It is essential to ask this question, and it will free the woman from a sense of guilt if she is truly not suited to the position.

- *Are you willing to make a two-year commitment?*

  As mentioned before, a two-year commitment allows for staggered terms and the training of new people. When setting up a board initially, it will be necessary to start with half of the members serving for either one year, or three. From then only one-half of the board will complete their term each year and that will provide needed continuity for the board.

When the woman expresses an interest, I make clear from the start that we are asking that the Women's Ministries Program take priority over her other activities outside her home and family responsibilities during her service on the board. Jesus taught that it was important to count the cost before making a commitment (Luke 14:28).

If she is involved in a parachurch organization, I always encourage her but suggest that serving on the Women's Ministries Board provides her with relationships with and ministry to women of her own church. I am grateful to these many groups that equip women in the Scripture and train them to serve. We are not in competition with them. Rather, we need to give these equipped women opportunity for significant ministry in the local church. We have many women who have invested their lives in our ministry, and I think it is significant that in the fourteen Women's Ministries

Boards I've served with, only three women ever repeated their service. This variety has resulted in continual development of new methods to accomplish our goals to equip and mentor women. We are always grooming leadership at every age. Each year there are a variety of ages on the board.

DIVERSITY

Not only do we enjoy a diversity of ages; we also strive to reach out with economic and educational diversity. Again we follow in this the example of Jesus. The twelve disciples came from a wide spectrum of society, from tax collectors to fishermen. Jesus called them to follow Him and to work together in a unity formed from diversity.

In today's church culture, we have women who have a wide range of educational and economic backgrounds. Many young women have high levels of education. A young lawyer whose limited practice from her home allowed her to care for her young family led one of our electives. Her elective was called "Legal Matter Chatter," dealing with common legal issues women face daily. Another woman, self-educated in the stock market, led another very popular elective called Stock Market 101.

We also utilize diverse levels of spiritual maturity. There are many places in the program where even a person recently coming to faith can serve effectively. I remember a neighbor of one of our women coming to the Bible study and when we asked for those interested in leading an elective, she volunteered to lead a step aerobics class, as she did this professionally. Since we were not certain of her spiritual maturity, we asked a mature leader to team with her and to handle the shepherding aspects of the class, to get to know her better and to minister to her. This young woman encouraged by nurturing support became one of our most enthusiastic members.

LADDER OF LEADERSHIP

In many ways Women's Ministries provides a ladder of leadership development. The beginning rungs include jobs, although important, where failure to complete them adequately would not destroy the program. As you move up the ladder, the level of responsibility grows and the impact of unfaithfulness or irresponsibility is greater. Sharing hostessing responsibilities with coffee and snacks or sharing committee responsibilities in planning events are good places to train and test your volunteers. As we just discussed, leading electives gives greater opportunity to observe faithfulness and can accommodate volunteers. However, other jobs, such as serving on the board and teaching responsibilities are those that need to be filled with women chosen rather than filled with untested volunteers.

If you think of these broad areas of service, you can see that in many places leadership can be entered by those willing to volunteer. However, the higher up on the ladder of responsibility, with the greater impact by the actions of that position, it is best to invite those who have demonstrated faithfulness in previous ways. This is similar to the way the Scripture indicates that deacons "must first be tested" before they assume that significant office (1 Timothy 3:10).

In addition the Scripture affirms that those who have been faithful in little will be given more (Luke 19:17). We can't miss if we follow this scriptural pattern.

Developing Leaders

Jesus again serves as our model of leadership in development. He gave the disciples real responsibility and the authority to accomplish what He asked them to do. This is one of the key ways to develop leadership—trust them with responsibility, give them appropriate authority, and require accountability.

DELEGATION

A transforming leader will delegate responsibility to others. She will encourage and affirm their efforts and seek to bring out the best in them. She won't be a perfectionist who thinks her way is the best way. She won't be jealous for recognition so that she must always occupy center stage. She will be ready to provide help to the person struggling beyond her giftedness by finding team members to assist her where she is weak.

> DELEGATION DEVELOPS PEOPLE,
> NOT PROGRAMS.

ACCOUNTABILITY IN SERVICE

Sometimes we have to confront a woman because of her way of handling her position. When I see a member of the board overburdened with responsibilities, I ask, "Are you delegating?"

If a woman responds, "It's easier to do it myself, and it gets done the way that I want it," I must remind her that our job as leaders is to provide others with the opportunity to use their gifts in a protected environment. When there is supervision and accountability, a person is programmed for success rather than failure. Not only that, but we lose the benefits of other women's creativity when we don't let them contribute.

Part of my job in helping a person learn to delegate might be to ask her to give me a list of committee heads under her assignment within a certain time frame, for example, two weeks. Delegation develops people, and that is one of our main goals in the Women's Ministries Program.

An Example

Recently I spoke at a Christmas banquet where they began a Women's Ministries Program along our guidelines. This was their Christmas dinner. Throughout the meal two of the leaders peppered me with questions. "How do you get women to volunteer? How do you get women to take responsibility? What do you do if they don't do their job?"

I discovered that the entire dinner, the cooking and the decorations, had fallen almost entirely on these two women. They were discouraged and burned out. I asked if they had committees for these different jobs. Yes, they had. What kinds of reports had they had on their progress?

Well, they had asked the various chairmen, "How is the dinner coming?"

"Fine," came back the answer.

However, at the last minute, one chairman became ill, and nothing had been done, so it fell to those two women to pick up the slack.

I suggested that in their follow-up they needed much more specific information. They needed the names of each person assigned to specific tasks. They needed to know exactly how much each one had completed or what her plans were at least one month prior to the event.

ACCOUNTABILITY IN TEACHING

Another important area of accountability concerns what is being taught. I heard one of our teachers, an avid pet lover, say in answer to a question during one of her lessons that she was sure there would be pets in heaven. She said it with humor, but a Bible teacher has an authority given by Scripture, and it concerned me. Words spoken from a podium impact the hearers greatly.

After praying about it, I made the opportunity to speak to her. First, I praised her for the lesson and all the insights she had shared. Then I asked her about her statement. What passage in Scripture supported it? I suggested that we must make a clear distinction between what we wish or hope to be true and what we know for certain the Bible teaches. She was very gracious, understood what I meant, and thanked me. I felt I was protecting her ministry as an effective teacher and protecting those who relied upon her teaching as well.

I always listen to tapes of teachers I have not personally heard. Once, upon hearing a tape of a woman recommended as a retreat speaker, I was mystified. She spent the first fifteen minutes telling jokes like a stand-up comedian. She hardly used any Scripture at all. Her entire message consisted of a potpourri of thoughts about many subjects. This kind of teaching would definitely not build our women spiritually. Don't ask speakers to come just because they are well known. Ask instead, "Do they teach God's Word? Do they make it relevant to our lives today?"

When we invite a woman to speak for Bible studies or for retreats or luncheons, we also ask her to include the gospel. We assume that there is usually someone in the audience who does not know the Lord. We always encourage our women to bring friends and neighbors.

AN EXAMPLE

We had a woman with an important position in Washington, D.C., speak at our Christmas luncheon. Since we had asked her to do so, she gave her own personal testimony. She shared how she came to faith in Christ and continued by telling us how her present, unique position stretched her as she trusted the Lord to overcome her fears and enable her to do her job well. Later over lunch I thanked her for giving the gospel so clearly. She told me she had never done it previously as a part of her message. She included it because we specifically asked her to, but she said she would make it a regular part of her messages in the future.

LOVING CONFRONTATION

Clear lines of authority and responsibility help develop leaders as well. Everyone involved in Women's Ministries activities is accountable to the board. The board is responsible to supervise every area and help wherever there is a need. But when someone is not doing her job, she must be confronted lovingly but firmly. The solution is not to do it for her, as the women trying to prepare the Christmas banquet did.

Most of us prefer to avoid confrontation. We don't want to hurt someone's feelings. We don't want people to go away mad. We don't want to discourage them from serving. We don't want them to say bad things about us.

But bear in mind, when God gives us spiritual responsibility for the welfare of others, we must be diligent to help them develop in various ways. Self-control is one of the stated areas in which Titus 2 instructs the older women to train the younger women. Helpful and specific follow-up, as well as using people in the area of their giftedness, provides opportunities for success.

WORKING RETREATS

Jesus and his disciples spent much time together. A working retreat provides time not only to develop leadership but to develop deeper relationships as well.

We select our board replacements for outgoing members by February. Then the new members coming on can work alongside the persons they are replacing and become familiar with their responsibilities. In early May we have an overnight retreat with the current board and the new members. We also invite past board chairmen for their input as well.

This is a working retreat. Before coming everyone is asked to revise her job description, bringing it up-to-date. We first take time for prayer and for some encouragement from the Bible. Then we review the entire year's program and consider such questions as these:

- What should we change?
- What should we continue?
- What works most effectively?
- What needs to be improved?
- What did we enjoy most?
- What should we add?
- What was most difficult?
- Who might be a good Bible teacher?
- What new women who have not served previously might we invite to serve on committees?
- What new areas of outreach or support groups might we consider?

We thoroughly discuss everything. We also plan the next year's calendar so that our schedule can be placed on the church calendar as soon as possible to avoid scheduling conflicts where we can.

EVALUATION AND FEEDBACK

This kind of continual evaluation and feedback, not only from the board but also from the entire body of women served by the Women's Ministries Program, strengthens our ministry. We build it into the process throughout. We are continually surveying for interest areas and evaluating the effectiveness of the various aspects of the programs.

We are committed to stay open to change whenever it seems we are losing our edge. I also seek feedback from the staff and pastors in my contacts with them. In this rapidly changing world, this kind of flexibility protects us from becoming obsolete.

INNOVATION

I like to think that we have created an atmosphere open to innovation. Many of our outreach and elective ministries have come when someone has an idea or burden. If she or someone else will head it, we are open to giving it a try.

There are just a few basic parameters. The ministry must be squarely based on biblical truth, and there must be someone willing to take responsibility for leading it.

We worship a creative God, and we are open to following His direction in our Women's Ministries Program.

MOVING PEOPLE TO CHANGE

"Moving people to change is the essence of leadership. Ten per cent of any group will be early adapters who respond eagerly to new ideas. At the other end will be the 10 percent who will never change. The 80 percent in between will move slowly in new directions." Women never cease to amaze me with the extent of their creativity and new ideas.

Every time we fill a board position with a new person, she brings new ideas and methods to her area. Each of us should have a realistic view of our own strengths and weaknesses, and our areas of interest and disinterest. Then we'll appreciate the creativity of others. We won't get stuck in the rut of doing the same things over and over. We'll drop programs that have run their course and start new ones as needs are expressed.

I have found that the way to lead women is to give them responsibility with guidelines. And within the framework of those guidelines she is free to be as creative as she can be. But she is also accountable to the leaders, the staff, and the board. She is not a loose cannon doing her own thing. There's a fine balance here. They are accountable, but as their leaders we are responsible to help them be the best they can be.

Supporting Leaders

Once again we can consider Jesus when we think of supporting those that we lead. Jesus offered His own presence as well as His concern for the well-being of His disciples. It was Jesus who saw a need for the disciples to "come apart and rest." Even when leaving, Jesus assured His disciples that He "would never leave them or forsake them." He will stand with His own to the end. That's support!

TEAM CONCEPT

It's essential to consciously serve as part of a team. If we see ourselves as a team, we'll maximize and use each other's strengths and support each other in our weaknesses. The job of leaders is to equip others to do the work of the ministry. We shouldn't put people just in learning experiences but put them in doing—achieving enables people to grow. That means we can't be prima donnas but rather playing coaches. The Women's Ministries Board at Northwest Bible Church serves as a team. Each member has her own responsibility, but everyone helps wherever they are needed.

It's surprising, but some people have to be taught to work with others. If there is not an atmosphere where each person's contribution is respected, people will not speak up and run the risk of ridicule or being ignored. We once had a person who had to comment on what everyone else offered. Her comments were mostly negative, and she caused a great deal of resentment and friction in what had previously been a good working board. Finally, the chairman took her aside and lovingly told her that she didn't have to assume the responsibility of passing judgment on every idea that was presented. That's good leadership—to lovingly yet firmly confront a person who is really hurting the dynamics of the whole group.

If you serve on a church staff either volunteer or salaried, each department should support and cooperate with the ministry of the others, even if it's just behind the scenes with no credit given! We mustn't be territorial!

RELATIONSHIPS

One of the most rewarding aspects of the work on the Women's Ministries Program is the development of deep, personal relationships with the women who work closely with me on the board. I believe it is important that the board members be welded together in love and friendship. We encourage this by meeting socially in addition to our regular board meetings.

We have dinner at one member's home several times each year with our husbands. The hostess provides the main dish, and each of us brings a dish to complete the meal. This evening together proves beneficial as it gives our husbands exposure to Women's Ministries. When they hear all that is happening and get to know the women their wives are working with, they are even more supportive of their wives' participation.

We also have a luncheon at Christmas. This allows a sweet time of fellowship without focusing or concentrating on business. We really enjoy having fun together. When members complete their two years of service on the board, many tell me how much they miss that unique fellowship.

Relationships are also developed among committees of Women's Ministries and within the small groups as well. These relationships strengthen the impact of the program.

REMOVING ROADBLOCKS

Peter Drucker has said, "At the heart of everything I have done has been the thought of enabling others, getting the roadblocks out of the way, out of their thinking and their systems, to enable them to become all that they can be." I like to see this function as a major part of my role, removing roadblocks to allow women to become all God designed them to be.

Part of that can be anticipating and heading off unnecessary offenses. For instance, when we decided to make aerobics a part of our Women's Ministries Program, I was aware there could be a potential offense from the clothing worn to the church for exercise. Below is a memo from me to all the ladies in the aerobics elective designed to head off unnecessary offense.

We understand that exercising requires different clothing from what one usually wears to church. But since the aerobics electives are an integral part of the Women's Ministries Program and we meet on the church campus where men are often present, we have a dress code that we ask you to comply with.

If you wear leotards or body suits, please wear loose shorts and a loose top over them. Sweat suits are fine. Just avoid tight or skimpy outfits that are not suitable here. The biblical word for the Christian woman is modesty! And that applies even to aerobics. Thanks for your cooperation—and happy aerobics!

Anticipating potential problems and heading them off is usually the better part of wisdom. This principle applies in many situations. The women sense your support in things like this; they understand that you are looking out for them.

ENCOURAGING AND AFFIRMING

Encouraging and affirming each woman in her area of strength helps avoid the dangerous pitfall of competition and comparison. The realization of our frailty also helps us to avoid comparing ourselves with others and competing with them (2 Corinthians 10:12).

Competition and comparison are such American pastimes that it's easy to slip into it in our service to the Lord. We women, especially, must be very careful about this. It's so easy to think:

- "She's a better teacher, but I'm a better homemaker."
- "She counsels better, but I'm a better cook."
- "She's such a big shot, being up front, but I get more done behind the scenes."
- "I wish I had her gifts!"

Comparisons and competition have no place in the ministry. God made us members of a body where each of us has her own function and place. God made us different on purpose! That eliminates any reason for competition. It's as silly as my eye competing with my ear for importance. This fact will free us to encourage others, to affirm them. Honest affirmation is not flattery. Flattery encourages manipulation, not growth. To affirm means simply appreciating and pointing out strengths we see in others. We encourage them to build on them. Affirmation really involves nothing more than paying attention to someone else, caring about her, and expressing our care to her.

I want to emphasize this. Focus on finding something good to say about people's efforts. Praise them honestly for a job well done. You can always praise someone's willingness to offer her participation. Even when you have to point out something that needs correction, start with something positive. Then when sharing the negative, offer specific help, suggestions for improvement, and coaching if necessary. For instance, if a woman has a hard time organizing a message, offer to go over her first draft with her. Show her how to make applications or do an outline or whatever she needs. That way, she knows you have her best interests at heart and you're not just being a critic. On the whole, be lavish with sincere praise. It builds confidence and develops loyalty. It has been said that every negative needs to be balanced with at least five positive observations.

NURTURING

Part of my role as minister to women is to be available to counsel and encourage women of the church, especially those in roles of leadership. This means I take an interest in them and their families and make myself available to them personally and by telephone.

Praise and encouragement must be a large part of your leadership philosophy. I remember a wise woman once told me about my children, "Try to catch them doing something right." The same thought applies to leadership development. Pay close attention to the work of your various board members and give them positive feedback on their work.

Another good habit to develop is to pass on positive comments by others to those who have done something especially well. If we would busy ourselves passing on the positive comments we hear, we could bury most of the irritating and discouraging negatives.

Nurturing isn't limited to just the board members, however. We hope it occurs throughout the program. Women find women's ministry to be a safe place, no matter how terrible their past or how heavy their guilt. For example, our abortion recovery group has been very successful in bringing healing to the women who have taken this ten-week course.

I have been asked to speak at a memorial service this group gives at the end of the series that gives dignity and personal worth to their unborn babies. I always stress that when God forgives sin, He removes it from us, out of reach, out of sight, out of mind, and out of existence. He cleanses our conscience and frees us to serve Him.

Some of these women later give testimonies before the group to encourage others who have experienced abortion to seek this help. Each time, several women respond by calling the telephone number of the leader. Since this group is confidential, a woman can feel safe sharing the secret and the shame of her abortion, perhaps for the first time.

I was particularly touched by something I heard. When one of the women who had taken the post-abortion course gave her testimony at Women's Ministries, I just hugged her spontaneously after she was finished. Later I heard that one of the other women who eventually took the course said she did so because of that hug. She said, "Then I knew it was safe to come."

SEASONS OF LIFE

There are also many variables for women to consider. There are seasons in our lives that affect our availability. Women can have it all. We just can't have it all at the same time!

Women leaders, of all people, understand the pressures on the mother of young children. We won't burden her with guilt because she's not doing as much as an empty nester. We'll remind her that God calls raising children a good work! (1 Timothy 5:10).

If aging parents need more attention, we'll encourage women with the truth that they are obeying the commandment to honor their parents. We are fragile human beings with just twenty-four hours a day, and different ages and states of health. Nurturing feminine leadership will be gentle and compassionate. In 1 Thessalonians 2:7–8, Paul described how he cared for them as a man. How much easier this gentleness of a nursing mother who cherishes her children should be for women, who have this ability naturally. We must encourage women to see all of life as ministry, with no division between sacred and secular. God does. Then when family and job pressures lessen and her time is freed up, a woman can assume more responsibility in church ministry. Throughout life we minister, just in different ways at different times.

> WOMEN CAN HAVE IT ALL.
> WE JUST CAN'T HAVE IT ALL AT THE SAME TIME!

FRUITFULNESS COMES FROM GOD

Fruitfulness comes from God (1 Corinthians 3:5–9). Administration is getting things done through people. Godly leadership will recognize that no one is indispensable. Our ministry mustn't be built around individual superstars. We all do different things at different times and in different ways. Sometimes all we can do is plant the seed. Sometimes, we water and water and water it. Sometimes we cultivate and water what someone else has planted. Sometimes we have the joy of reaping.

The interesting thing is that the way the seed grows is a mystery. No one knows how growth happens. As someone has said, the parable of the seed in Mark 4:26–29 is meant to "encourage the discouraged and restrain the impatient. Sow the seed, wait and sleep!" Our responsibility is to always be investing our lives in the lives of others to encourage their growth in the Lord. But no matter what we may do, God is the only one who can make things grow. God is the only one who can make *people* grow.

DON'T BE A "FIXER"

Let me mention an inherent pitfall we must avoid as women leaders. Our nurturing character tempts us to want to fix everything. We can't! We must be careful to shift a person's dependence on us to dependence on the Lord. Obedience to God's Word and reliance on God's Spirit brings growth to maturity for anyone. It's our job to teach God's Word and to model godly living. Then we must leave the growth to God. We can encourage others and affirm that God is the life giver.

Just a Garment

Richard Halverson shared these thoughts on becoming Chaplain of the United States Senate. "I felt like a non-person, a mascot to one of the most powerful political bodies in the world. I wondered what I was doing there."

That evening he read the words of Jesus: "All authority in heaven and on earth has been given to me. And surely I am with you always." Then he realized, "I am a garment which Jesus Christ wears every day to do what He wants to do in the United States Senate. I don't need power; my weakness is an asset. If Christ is in me, what more do I need?"

You and I are the garment Jesus wears in ministry to women. He uses us in our weakness so that His excellent power is displayed.

P a r t   F i v e

GATHERING A
BOUQUET OF FLOWERS

*He produces a crop, yielding a hundred,
sixty or thirty times what was sown.*

MATTHEW 13:23

Thirteen

EXPECTED AND
EXPERIENCED RESULTS

Dolores's bright eyes danced as she began to share with me how God had led her to accept our invitation to serve on the board as hospitality coordinator. "If anyone had told me four years ago that I would have been able or willing to serve on the Women's Ministries Board, I would have told them they were crazy!"

Her comments didn't really surprise me, but once again I experienced the joy in seeing how God works in the lives of women when they are given an opportunity to grow and develop within the local church in the very way He designed for them.

Dolores had come to the Women's Ministries Program as a quiet and retiring woman. She was new in her faith and unsure of any way that she could contribute to the lives of others. Now, only four years later, she was excitedly sharing the outline she had prepared to present from the platform to over two hundred women who were coming to our Women's Ministries Seminar.

Dolores related her excellent ideas about hospitality, how God had answered her specific prayers for such practical things as centerpieces and how much she had grown in learning to depend on God in all the little details of life.

She had taken one of our elective classes on hospitality in the home. She told how she began to sense that God was drawing her to a greater ministry of hospitality. At first she thought about it only in the context of her home. She made plans to invite various people for meals and was praying about other directions that God would have about hospitality. It was about that time that I called her to ask if she would consider serving in the board position as hospitality coordinator. Her affirmative answer was quick in coming, and she joined the board. Her service in that position was so effective that I had asked her to share that job description at the Women's Ministries Seminar.

This blooming of potential spiritual growth is the bouquet of results that I have seen repeated over and over again. Each year I experience the joy of seeing women grow as they exercise their God-given gifts in service to the body of Christ. This same potential is available through you and the women of your church.

God created women with vast stores of creative talent and energy. They will invest and develop it somewhere. How delightful it is when it can be channeled to the benefit of the work of God through the church. I am thankful for many parachurch organizations that have tapped this creative energy and used it to reach out into our world. They have demonstrated the impact that women can make when they commit their lives to God and His work. However, I am convinced that we need to provide this same opportunity of significant ministry for women within the local church as well.

Here are just a few typical notes I've received about the impact of the Women's Ministries Program on the lives of women. You have women just like these in your church.

Dear Vickie,

I consider myself a typical "Dallas Mom" trying to raise small children while striving to grow personally and to be ever fulfilled in order to give my very best to my husband, children, and those around me. Due to the fast pace we live and such a mobile society, I have found raising children can be a very lonesome job. Personal fulfillment also seems hard to attain. The Women's Ministries Program has more than satisfied three empty areas in my life:

1. Intellectual stimulation
2. Social interaction
3. Small prayer-support groups

Plus I'm happy to be there on Tuesdays! It's a wonderful program that should meet many needs of a large number of busy, happy, but lonesome and/or unfulfilled women here in Dallas.

Dear Vickie,

Thanks for your tireless work in "feeding His sheep." I love Women's Ministries and look forward to learning something new about God every Tuesday. Your efforts are reaching far beyond NBC. As you disciple us, we, in turn, disciple others. I checked out your tape on 1 Corinthians 12 and taught it to a group of ten in my home.

They all expressed how it impacted them. They also have loved learning about spiritual gifts and are convicted to find opportunities to serve the church-at-large as well as their own local church!

Thanks for making a difference in my life!

As I mentioned earlier, we have available the resource of various types of counselors to assist with problems that surface in the Women's Ministries Program.

In the context of loving relationships between women, embarrassing and difficult problems are shared. With the structure of support and accountability of the Women's Ministries program, these women can be encouraged, loved, and prayed for. Also, it is often possible to refer them to others who can help in specific areas. The following note is from a single woman who had maxed out on six credit cards. She was over her head and longing for help. We referred her to a couple in our church that counsels those with financial problems. Her life was changed.

Dear Vickie,

Just wanted to thank you for referring me to Don and Suzie. They have been terrific. They are helping me make a spending plan, and it all makes sense, even to me! It's going to be tough, but I feel blessed to have a chance to learn my lesson.

I said earlier that I believe that when women minister to women the entire church is blessed and benefited. Conversely, the lack of a Women's Ministries Program can leave a church without all the warmth and love women can bring to a congregation. Truly, a church without a vital Women's Ministries Program is like a home without a mother. Older women have walked in life where the younger women are walking, and they can make a difference in significant decisions the younger women make and directions they take. God has given us this work for the good of the next generation. We dare not neglect it.

Part Six

AN ALMANAC
OF RESOURCES

Appendix One

A PROPOSAL TO ESTABLISH A WOMEN'S MINISTRY PRESENTED TO THE GOVERNING BODY OF A LOCAL CHURCH

Below is an outline of the initial proposal presented to the elders of Northwest Bible Church to enlist their support. The women prepared and duplicated the report, and a copy was presented to each elder at a special dinner hosted by the committee.

Page 1 The cover sheet was an attractive shade of pink with the logo for the Women's Ministries Program that one of the women designed. You can develop your own, or simply use the title "Women's Ministries."

Page 2 Executive Summary. This page summarized the result of the survey of the women. Also included was a statement of the needs, several points about the proposal, and the action points requested.

Page 3 This page listed the names of the women on the working committee, as well as a list of the various women who had served in an advisory capacity.

Page 4 This page carried an organizational chart showing the various aspects of the Women's Ministries Program and how they related to one another. It showed how existing ministries were included in the overall transition plan.

Page 5 This page listed the "Proposed Schedule for the Weekly Program" as well as the anticipated dates for sessions in the upcoming year.

Page 6 This page listed the Bible teaching planned for the upcoming sessions, as well as a list of the various kinds of electives, together with their leaders.

Page 7   This page carried a job description for the requested position of Minister to Women, including qualifications and responsibilities.

Page 8   This page was a letter from the pastor to the elders indicating his support of the program as proposed by the committee.

Page 9   The final pages contained quotes from well-known people and from some of our own women about the importance of a Women's Ministries Program. I have included those quotations following the organizational chart.

Page 10 This page was a matching cover sheet in pink.

ORGANIZATIONAL CHART FOR A WOMEN'S MINISTRIES PROGRAM

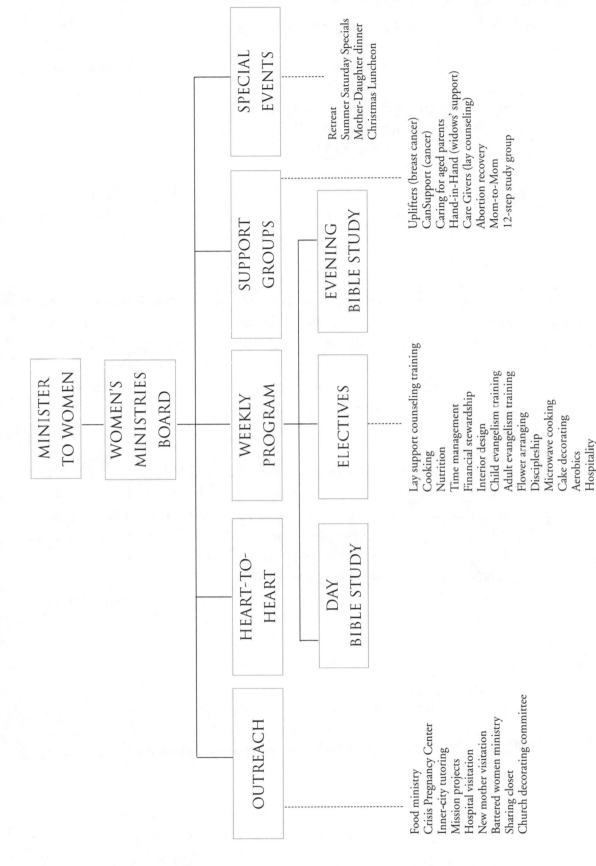

MINISTER TO WOMEN

WOMEN'S MINISTRIES BOARD

OUTREACH

Food ministry
Crisis Pregnancy Center
Inner-city tutoring
Mission projects
Hospital visitation
New mother visitation
Battered women ministry
Sharing closet
Church decorating committee

HEART-TO-HEART

DAY BIBLE STUDY

WEEKLY PROGRAM

ELECTIVES

Lay support counseling training
Cooking
Nutrition
Time management
Financial stewardship
Interior design
Child evangelism training
Adult evangelism training
Flower arranging
Discipleship
Microwave cooking
Cake decorating
Aerobics
Hospitality
Calligraphy
Quilting
Crafts of all kinds

SUPPORT GROUPS

EVENING BIBLE STUDY

Uplifters (breast cancer)
CanSupport (cancer)
Caring for aged parents
Hand-in-Hand (widows' support)
Care Givers (lay counseling)
Abortion recovery
Mom-to-Mom
12-step study group

SPECIAL EVENTS

Retreat
Summer Saturday Specials
Mother-Daughter dinner
Christmas Luncheon

In Support of Change . . .

"There has been a dynamic change in women's lives. . . . Their time scheduling is very important, so just a Bible study format is not enough. Women's groups are struggling all over the country. We need to be much more diverse to meet everyone's needs. . . . No one needs just another meeting."
Jeanne Hendricks

"I agree wholeheartedly that it was wise for you to discontinue the old format for a year. I haven't seen that format work well for a long time. It takes something specialized to make women come to something apart from their husbands."
Anne Ortland

"A century ago, women cooked together, canned together, washed clothes at the creek together, prayed together. . . . Alas, the situation is very different today. The extended family has disappeared, depriving the wife of that source of security and fellowship. . . . The difference between them can be seen in the breakdown in relationships between women. Instead, you must achieve a network of women friends with whom you can talk, laugh, gripe, dream, and recreate."
Dr. James Dobson, *Straight Talk to Men and Their Wives*

"Stuart Briscoe stated in an article in *Moody Monthly* in February 1983 entitled, 'The Biblical Woman, We've Buried a Treasure,' 'We know the Holy Spirit gifts all believers, including women, for the upbuilding of the church and the glory of God.

"'The Master has great numbers of female servants. . . . They seem to have a great heart for the Lord; they love to study the Word of God and are eager to pray.

"'But even though they are so numerous and so interested, the full force of cumulated talents doesn't seem to have been released. So great has been the burial that some of us think the greatest wasted resource in the church is women-power. . . . A talent is a terrible thing to waste.'"
From *Northwest Women*

D. T. expressed concern for lack of unity within the body. She stated that she has never felt that she and her husband were an integral part of Northwest, and had even attended other churches, but had always come back because of the teaching. She expressed excitement about the proposed plan because it offered a solution.

"If the women of the church were united, there's no end as to what might happen."
G. D., from Northwest Bible Church

Appendix Two

RESOURCES AVAILABLE
FROM TITUS 2:4 MINISTRIES

Two Videos Are Available in VHS

Organizing an Effective Women's Ministry
The Feminine Face of Leadership

Audio Lesson Tapes by Vickie Kraft

God's Power for Our Inadequacy
(The Life of Moses; 24 tapes)

Timeless Solutions for 20th Century Problems
(Study of 1 Corinthians; 23 tapes)

Victorious Living in a Dying Culture
(Study of Romans; 18 tapes)

Character Study—Life of Joseph
(8 tapes)

Godly Living in an Ungodly World
(Study of Daniel; 9 tapes)

Born Free (Sample questions follow)
(Study of Galatians; 8 tapes)

To Know Him . . . To Be Like Him
(Study of Gospel of Mark; 16 tapes)

Jesus Christ: God Revealed
(9 tapes)

Winning God's Approval (Sample questions follow)
(Study of the characters in Hebrews 11; 9 tapes)

Overcoming Emotional Obstacles to Spiritual Maturity
(20 tapes) Studies of biblical characters who struggled with guilt, regret, fear, worry, forgiveness, anger, envy, rejection, materialism, inferiority, pride, disappointment, grief, loneliness, and selfishness. We learn that God is the great healer of our emotions.
There is one lesson per tape.

Individual tapes may be purchased by mail for $5.00 for each by mailing a check to:

Titus 2:4 Ministries
P. O. Box 797566
Dallas, TX 75379-7566

Sample Questions for Bible Studies

WINNING GOD'S APPROVAL

Hebrews 11:4

QUESTIONS—LESSON 2

1. Read the book of Hebrews through this week. Underline key words such as *better, blood, faith, High Priest, eternal, let us,* and *Son.*
2. Read Genesis 4. In what ways were Cain and Abel the same? In what ways were they different?
3. How did their worship differ?
4. List Cain's downward progression.
5. Why did he kill Abel? (Matthew 23:35; 1 John 3:12)
6. Was Cain a believer who sinned, or an unbeliever? (1 John 3:12)
7. What evidence is there that Cain belonged to the evil one? (John 8:44)
8. Count how many times the word *brother* is used in Genesis 4 and in 1 John 3:12. Why do you think this is emphasized?
9. What do we learn of the character of God in His dealings with Cain?
10. What two basic approaches to God do the two offerings present?

DIGGING DEEPER

1. What is implied by the statement in Hebrews 11, "By faith Abel offered a better sacrifice"? What is necessary for faith? (Romans 10:17). Suggest the significance of Genesis 4:2–4 in this regard.
2. What did the offering of animals teach the offerer about God, man, sin, and salvation?
3. What did the blood of Abel speak out for? (Hebrews 12:24) What is the "better word" of which the blood of Christ speaks? (1 John 1:7; John 1:29; Hebrews 9:12, 14, 22; 10:19)
4. What is the significance of the first man born murdering the second in light of Romans 5:12–21?
5. How would you describe the "way of Cain"? (Jude 11)

APPLICATION QUESTIONS

1. What does 1 John 3:12 tell us about the attitude of unbelievers toward believers? Why is it important to understand this basic fact to have a proper worldview? Does this passage help you to understand a difficult relationship you may be experiencing now?

2. What are some of the reasons we can begin to hate other believers? If we have a "just" cause and the one who harmed us gives no sign of repentance or desire for forgiveness, are we justified in harboring resentment?

   a. What must we do? (Matthew 18:15–17; Ephesians 4:32)

   b. Why is it necessary? (Hebrews 12:14)

   c. Who gets the advantage when we don't forgive?

   d. Is there someone in your life now that you are bitter toward? What will you do about it on the basis of this lesson?

   e. If the situation doesn't change, how can you change? (1 Thessalonians 5:1–8, 4:1; Philippians 4:8).

   f. How can forgiving be done by faith?

3. How does a person today attain a right relationship with God? What works does she have to do? How can anyone know that she will continue in that relationship? What does one have to do to stay there? (Ephesians 2:8–10; John 10:27–29; John 6:28,29; John 5:24).

Hebrews 11:30–31

QUESTIONS—LESSON 6

1. Why was God giving Israel the land of Canaan? (Genesis 12:1; 15:12–20; 28:13–15; Exodus 3:7–8, 16–17)

2. What did God want to teach these people by doing this? Remember, they had lived for 400 years in a nation that was grossly idolatrous. (Deuteronomy 4:32–40; esp. 36–38)

3. What did the king's orders in Joshua 2:2–3 indicate about the knowledge of the people of Jericho concerning Israel and her future? See also Joshua 9:9–11, 24.

4. What was the state of the morale in Jericho? (Joshua 2:9,11; 6:1). How does this confirm God's promises in Deuteronomy 1:21, 29, 31?

5. Read carefully Joshua 2:9–13. What did Rahab know about Israel's history? How long before had the Red Sea been crossed? (Exodus 14; Deuteronomy

2:7) How long before had Sihon and Og been conquered? (Deuteronomy 2:26–3:11)

6. What did Rahab specifically say she believed about the God of Israel? What is impressive about her faith? Could anyone else in Jericho have come to the same conclusions?

7. How did she demonstrate her faith? What risk was she taking? (Joshua 2:4–7, 12–13,21; James 2:25)

8. How was her faith rewarded? (Joshua 2:12–13, 27–21; 6:22–24; Matthew 1:5)

9. What conclusions do you draw from Rahab's inclusion in the genealogy of Jesus Christ? (Matthew 1:5). How did Jesus treat immoral women when He was here on earth? (John 4; John 8:1–11)

DIGGING DEEPER

1. How do you reconcile Rahab's disobeying and lying to her king when compared to the principle stated in Romans 13:1–6? See also 2 Samuel 19:11–17; Exodus 1:15–20; Acts 4:19; 5:29.

2. Note the word used to describe the rest of the people of Jericho, *disobedient*. What were they disobedient regarding? (Romans 1:18–32; 2:14–15) For the same concept see Ephesians 2:2; 5:6, 12; Titus 3:3; and Romans 1:5.

3. What happened between the episode of the spies and the conquest of Jericho? (Joshua 3). With this knowledge, when the people of Jericho saw the army marching around their walls for seven days, what could they have done? (Joshua 2:9–14). See also 9:9–11, 24.

4. What does the mention of this woman three times in the New Testament tell us about the grace of God and the nature of sin? Study Romans 3:9–26 and list.

APPLICATION QUESTIONS

1. Do you feel that some sins in your past or present are so terrible that they can't be forgiven, or that you are unworthy to serve God? How does the story of Rahab encourage you? Read Colossians 3:1–17 to see how God views you and your responsibilities as His child. Memorize Colossians 3:1–4.

2. Acts 26:17–18 and 1 Thessalonians 1:9 reveal that a drastic change took place in the lives of these early believers, as it did with Rahab. Has your life changed substantially since you trusted Christ, or do you have a foot in both worlds? What do you need to stop doing? To start doing?

3. Notice how the total person was involved in Rahab's faith: her mind had facts (Joshua 2:8–11), her emotions reacted (2:11), her will made a decision, and she acted (2:12–14). This is always involved in true faith. It's not enough to know about Jesus Christ, but with an act of our will we must personally trust Him as Savior. Have you done this? This also applies to the process of growth as a Christian—the will must decide and act.

BORN FREE

Galatians 4:1–31

QUESTIONS—LESSON 5

1. (Vv. 1–7) What would be the differences in the positions, privileges, and responsibilities between a mature son and heir, and a slave in a household?

2. (V. 7) God has made us His heirs. Study the following passages to get some insight about this inheritance: Romans 8:16,17; Ephesians 3:6–12; Hebrews 1:2; 1 Peter 1:3–6; 3:7. Do you actually think of yourself as God's heir? How would that change your view toward life and goals here on earth?

3. (V. 4) What is the purpose of Christ's redemption here? Compare with 1:4, 3:14. What do this verse and John 1:15; 3:16; 1 John 4:14; and Hebrews 2:4 tell us about Jesus' humanity and its purpose?

4. (Vv. 8–10) What were the Galatians and all Gentiles formerly slaves to? (1 Corinthians 12:2; 10:19, 20) By placing themselves under the law for sanctification, what were they in danger of being enslaved to now?

5. (Vv. 12–20) Paul was like a father in the way he treated the Galatians. What principles for discipling children can we learn from this section?

6. (V. 16) This verse reveals the risk we face when we confront someone with the truth. Has this ever happened to you? What did you do as a result?

7. (Vv. 17–18) What were the motives of the false teachers?

8. (V. 19) What was Paul's goal for his ministry? What should be your goal for yourself and other believers? (Romans 8:29; Ephesians 4:13–15; Colossians 1:27) How can you accomplish this?

9. (Vv. 21–31) Read Genesis 16:1–16 and 21:1–21 for background. What words are used to describe Hagar and Sarah? (22, 23, 30, 31) What does each represent? (24)

10. (V. 29) What is always the attitude of legalism toward grace?

11. (Vv. 30–31) What is Paul saying about law and grace, works and faith, and bondage and freedom here?

12. (Vv. 28–31) Whose child are you?

13. Since you were born *free*, what impact should that make on your concept of living to please God and growing to maturity? (1 Thessalonians 4:1) How can you achieve this goal? (Romans 6:6–18) What is God's part? What is your part?

14. Can you think of a sin you are enslaved to? Take the steps in Romans 6:11–14 and trust the Spirit of God to set you free in this specific area.

GOD'S WOMEN

Why Do Bad Things Happen to Good People?

QUESTIONS—2 KINGS 4:1–7

1. What was the spiritual condition of the Northern Kingdom, Israel, as exemplified by her kings? (2 Kings 1:1–3; 3:1–3)

2. What do we know about the widow's husband from verse 1? Write down all you can deduce from these brief statements.

3. What do you learn about the "company (or sons) of the prophets"? Who were they? What did they do? Who were their leaders? (See 1 Kings 20:35; 2 Kings 2:3, 5, 7, 15; 4:1, 38; 5:22; 6:1; 9:1)

4. The Mosaic Law provided for paying off debts by working (Leviticus 25:39–41) How did God limit this practice?

5. What responsibility did God place on the entire community regarding widows and orphans? (Exodus 22:22, 23; Deuteronomy 14:28–29; 24:19–21) Did Israel obey God in this? (Isaiah 1:17, 23; 10:1)

6. What does God promise to do? (Deuteronomy 10:18; Psalm 68:5)

7. Why did the widow come to Elisha? What was especially pathetic about her situation?

8. What does Elisha's response tell us about him? (2 Kings 4:2a)

9. What do you deduce from the fact that he used what she had as a resource? Compare Exodus 4:1–5; Mark 6:35–44. Write down a principle that you can derive from this. Can you now make a specific application of this principle to your own life?

10. List all the things that Elisha commanded the widow to do. Why did he have her ask her neighbors for jars?

11. What impact do you think this incident had on her sons? In what practical ways can you show your children what God is like?

12. What had she asked Elisha's help for? What did she actually receive?

13. How did this destitute widow become an influence in her day? In our day?

14. How did God "defend her cause"? (Deuteronomy 10:18) Compare 1 Kings 17:1–24 and note the similarities.

15. What is our responsibility today to the orphan and widow? (1 Timothy 5:16; James 1:27). What do they need besides material provisions? Is there someone you can provide any of this for *this week?*

16. What does God expect of us as women in our homes, church, and community? (Romans 12:1–21; Galatians 6:9–10) Study these passages and ask God to reveal a specific area where He wants you to be obedient to Him as you reach out to meet someone's need.

Appendix Three

INSTRUCTIONS FOR SUPPORT GROUPS AND OUTREACH MINISTRIES

Uplifters

Uplifters is a support ministry through which women who have had breast cancer support current breast cancer patients and their families. We are available to ladies who have discovered a breast lump and need to talk. We answer questions pertaining to breast cancer and breast disease. An Uplifter will talk with anyone from our church as well as the community. We meet only as needed. On occasion, Uplifters will eat lunch together. At this time, we support each other through our friendships and our prayers. This is a very special group to each of us who are directly involved. Anyone who has had breast cancer and who desires to serve others is welcome to join.

Areas of outreach are:

1. One-on-one support ministry—described above.
2. CanSupport—A cancer support group for women who have experienced cancer. This group is open to ladies from our church and our community. CanSupport meets monthly on the second Tuesday during lunch at 12:15 P.M. till everyone leaves. The ladies bring a sack lunch to eat, talk, and pray for each other and others who are unable to attend. CanSupport chose to meet during the lunch hour so that those who work can attend.

3. Yearly Screening Mammography—A local hospital-based mammography mobile unit comes to campus at Northwest Bible Church during our Women's Ministries Tuesday morning and Wednesday night sessions. Mammograms done through this mobile unit cost less than through a private physician and are more convenient.

4. Caring and Sharing, Women-to-Women—Uplifters offered this class one year during the Tuesday morning Women's Ministries electives. Our purpose was to learn appropriate caring and sharing techniques for difficult circumstances. These biblically based principles were taught by women who had experienced various difficulties. Some of the subjects discussed were coping with elderly parents, helping the chronically ill person, and the death of a loved one.

5. Uplifters will assist any church starting its own group. Please ask us.

RESOURCES FOR UPLIFTERS

Pamphlets:
    Mom Is Very Sick: Here's How to Help, by Wendy Bergren
    My Child Is Very Sick: Here's How to Help, by Sissy Gaes
    Order from Focus on the Family, Colorado Springs, CO 80995.

Books:
    When the Doctor Says It's Cancer, by Mary Beth Moster. Available from local bookstores or Tyndale House Publishers.
    God's Faithfulness in Trials and Testings, by Sandy Edmonson. Order from Missionary Crusader International, 2451 34th St., Lubbock, TX 79411-1635.
    Then the Sun Came Up, by Helen Palston Tucker. Star Books, Inc., 408 Pearson St., Wilson, NC 27893.
    My Book for Kids with Cancer, by Jason Gaes. Melius and Peterson Publishing, Inc., 524 Citizens Bldg., Aberdeen, SD 57401.
    A Spiritual Journey Through Breast Cancer, by Judy Asti (Chicago: Moody, 2002).

Cassette
    Surviving Breast Cancer; Dr. James Dobson and panel. Focus on the Family, Colorado Springs, CO 80995.

Healing the Hurts of Abortion

Considering that millions of babies have been aborted since abortion was legalized in the United States, there are many women and men within our churches who have been hurt by abortion. The purpose of our ministry is to become a Good Samaritan to those hurting. Through a ten-week Bible study we help them recognize how God sees abortion and recognize their need to confess their part in the abortion(s). We then show them through the Bible God's grace and forgiveness, that God forgives them, and that they need to forgive themselves and others.

We allow these victims of abortion to give their baby(ies) identity and dignity and to grieve the loss of their babies. Throughout our class, we provide love, prayer, support, and encouragement. Each person attending our class has her own "caretaker" who ministers to her individual needs.

We use the curriculum "Healing the Hurts of Abortion," written by Ken Freeman of Last Harvest Ministries, a pro-life ministry here in Dallas (P. O. Box 462192, Garland, TX 75046). We announce our class at Women's Ministries, in the adult Sunday school classes, and in the church bulletin. Also, Ken Freeman refers women to us who have called his hot-line number requesting help in dealing with the hurts of their abortion(s).

It is wonderful to see women returning to the Lord as this Bible study presents God's truths and surrounds the people we are ministering to with God's love.

Mom-to-Mom

GOALS AND OBJECTIVES:

Goal: To encourage mothers of young children
Objectives: Information/Program
     Practical
     Spiritual
    Prayer and Sharing Outreach/Publicity
    Fellowship /Friendship
    Internal Communications/Prayer Chain Nursery
    Food
    Service to Others

PROGRAM CHAIRMAN AND COORDINATOR
OF STEERING COMMITTEE

Plan stimulating programs, spiritual and practical

Set up room, coordinate with the scheduling secretary and the church calendar, turn in room arrangement

Introduce the speaker

Program time: 10:00–11:00

Plan transition into prayer time with prayer and sharing leader

Write a thank-you note to the speaker

PRAYER AND SHARING

Begins at 11:00

Promote informal, nonthreatening prayer and sharing

Plan creative ways for entire group to share in an effective and nurturing manner

HOSTESS

Be available to greet members and guests at 9:15

Permanent nametags and signs

Assist with attendance records and membership roster updates:
  Follow-up
  Coordinate with prayer chain leaders

Plan informal fellowship and introduction from 9:15–10:00. Begin the program at 10:00 sharp!! with program chairman

Plan an informal function once a year for spouses

Function as contact person for new members and visitors

SECRETARY

Liaison with hostess to update membership rosters

Mail: Calendar
          Program Plans
          Membership Roster
          Prayer Chain

Internal communications among committee members

Maintain membership roster

Have calendar, membership roster, and prayer chains available at the meetings

CONTACT COORDINATOR

Organize prayer chain
Coordinate prayer chain leaders
    Duties: Monthly nursery and lunch count
                        Maintain contact with group
                        Follow up absences, illnesses, needs
Activate the prayer chain as the need arises
Keep contact group roster current, add and delete names as needed
Inform membership of the functions of the prayer chain

OUTREACH/PUBLICITY

Liaison with Women's Ministries Board
Purpose is to inform church body of our ministry
Update announcements and information in church bulletin, church calendar,
    church newsletter, and Women's Ministries brochures
Keep informed of upcoming programs and changes
Coordinate with program director and secretary

NURSERY

Liaison with contact group leaders
Liaison with church nursery staff for:
    number of nursery workers needed
    number of actual reservations
    exact dates and times of meetings for the year
Nursery coordinator's name and phone number must be on all publications;
    nursery reservations are to be stressed
Encourage participation in Women's Ministries

FOOD

Organize luncheons on Tuesdays (3) and one picnic
Organize brunches on Wednesdays with prayer chain leaders
Delegate luncheon preparations to group members
Set up food service area
Supervise cleanup of food service and meeting areas

SERVICE

Dallas Life Foundation—coordinate cake, cupcakes, and drink for birthday party one day a month

Visitation to New Mothers:

Coordinate with outreach/publicity in supplying visitation committee with information about our meetings

Coordinate with hostess and secretary about new mothers who may be visiting our group

Coordinate new mother visitation within moms' group

Assist coordinator of new mother visitation ministry in keeping a current list of pregnant ladies/due date roster

Suggested Reading List for Twelve-Step Groups

Adult Children of Alcoholics, Janet G. Woitiz, Health Comm.; also G. K. Hall (large print)

After the Tears, Jane Middleton-Moz and Lorie Dwinell, Health Comm.

Beyond Codependency, Melody Beattie, HarperCollins

The Big Book, Alcoholics Anonymous

Codependent No More, Melody Beattie, Hazelden; also HarperCollins; also Walker (large type)

Cutting Loose, Howard M. Halpern, Fireside (Simon & Schuster Trade); also Bantam (1989 ed.)

The Dance of Anger, Harriet Goldhor Lerner, HarperCollins

Dying for a Drink, Anderson Spickard and Barbara R. Thompson, Word

Facing Codependency, Pia Mellody et al., Harper San Francisco

Getting Them Sober, vols. 1, 2, 3, Toby Rice Drews, Bridge

Grandchildren of Alcoholics, Ann Smith, Health Comm.

Healing for Damaged Emotions, David Seamands, Victor

I'll Quit Tomorrow, Vernon E. Johnson, Harper San Francisco

Inside Out, Larry Crabb, NavPress

Intervention, Vernon E. Johnson, Johnson Inst.

Love Is a Choice, Frank B. Minirth and Paul D. Meier, Thomas Nelson

One Day at a Time in Al-Anon, Al-Anon Family Group Headquarters

Peoples' Pharmacy, rev. ed., Joe Graedon, St. Martins

Permission to Be Precious, Pia Mellody (tapes)

The Pleasers, Kevin Leman, Dell

Recovery: A Guide for Adult Children of Alcoholics, Hebert L. Gravitz and Julie D. Bowden, Fireside (Simon & Schuster Trade)

Sin: Overcoming the Ultimate Deadly Addiction, Keith Miller, HarperCollins

Struggle for Intimacy, Janet Woitiz, Health Comm.

The Twelve Steps: A Spiritual Journey, Recovery (workbook)

Twelve Steps for Christians, Recovery

Women Who Love Too Much, Robin Norwood, Pocket; also Tarcher (hardback; distrib. by St. Martins)

Hospitality Volunteers for Newcomers

WELCOMING NEWCOMERS

Thank you for volunteering to help us welcome visitors to (Northwest Bible Church). The interest visitors have in returning to (Northwest) is very often heavily influenced by their perception of our concern for them and willingness to reach out to them. A friendly telephone call during the week after their Sunday visit to (Northwest) is a very important way of saying, "You are special to us!" With this letter, I am also giving you a packet of information to help you answer any questions that may arise during your telephone conversations. I will use a rotation system for asking you to call, so you may hear from me only every month or so.

Following are a few suggestions to help you make your calls more meaningful. Remember that these are just suggestions; use your own words and feel free to add or take away from what I have listed.

Please make it a priority to call those on your list as soon as possible. Calling soon after their visit conveys that they are a priority to us and also gives us the opportunity to answer visitors' questions when they are still clear in their minds. I will try to get the names in the mail to you the day I receive them.

Again, thank you for your willingness to help in this important ministry. Please direct questions, problems, or any positive/negative comments gathered during your phone conversation to me (name and telephone number of coordinator).

1. Begin by introducing yourself, saying that you are from (Northwest Bible Church) and asking, "Have I caught you at a time that you can talk for a few minutes?" If not, call back at a more convenient time.

2. Express appreciation for their visit; in your own way, let them know that you are glad that they joined us on Sunday, e.g., "We're glad that you came last Sunday."

3. All visitors are sent a letter from the pastor, and they are usually called by another staff pastor, who explains general church information and answers questions. The names that are sent to you are only those of women who live in the (Dallas) area, because our primary reason for calling is to provide additional information about Women's Ministries and to extend an invitation to join us. Ask, "Are you aware of our Women's Ministries Program, which provides a Bible study followed by special elective classes on Tuesday mornings or Wednesday evenings? Would you like more information about it?"

4. It is possible that a staff member may not have contacted them, so they may have additional questions about the church. Feel free to answer any questions in this area. You may ask, "Can I answer any questions about our church for you?" If the answer is "No" or "Not really," you might proceed with a few more direct questions, e.g., "Were you able to find your way around all right?" "Do you have any questions about the Sunday school classes?" You might ask, "Did you have any trouble finding a parking place?" The Parking Posse will direct them to a special visitors' parking area if they are aware that the person is

a visitor. If they did have trouble parking, suggest that they tell a member of the Parking Posse that they are visiting, if they choose to visit again. You might also ask, "Are you aware of the Wednesday night programs for children and adults that begin with a dinner at 5:15 P.M.?"

Suggestions for Hospital Visitation

1. Please call the patient before the visit to decide on a convenient time.
2. It is not necessary to take gifts, but a pretty card, a simple flower, or inspirational reading material would be nice (*Guideposts, Daily Walk,* or *Daily Bread*). Tapes may be borrowed from the church and picked up on your next visit (Sunday's sermon, Christian music).
3. Please don't visit when you are feeling "down"; the patient usually needs an uplifting experience. Being a good listener is very important, as the woman you are calling on may wish to talk.
4. Make note of any special needs of the person, such as requests for Communion or a pastoral visit. Will there be a need for future visits from you when the patient goes home, or would an occasional phone call be sufficient?
5. You may wish to ask the following:
   a. "Is there anything I can do for you, such as write a note or run an errand?"
   b. "Is there any Bible passage that has a special meaning for you that I could read or that we could read together?" (Psalm 23; Philippians 4:6–7)
   c. "May we pray before I go?" A very short prayer is fine.
6. Please keep your visits short, perhaps just 3–5 minutes, with 15 minutes the maximum, unless the patient asks that you stay longer.
7. Please telephone the coordinator after each hospital visit, so that she can keep a record of who has been seen and can pass along any special needs that the patient has.
8. If you are visiting someone who has returned home from the hospital, you might remember the casseroles available in the freezer at the church.
9. We will try to have occasional meetings of our visitation committee, so that we may share helpful suggestions with each other. Please feel free to recommend books, pamphlets, or favorite Scripture to enable all of us to be more effective witnesses for Christ.

Tutoring in an Inner-city High School

The women at Northwest Bible Church have long been involved in West Dallas, an inner-city public housing community. Women have participated in various capacities through a local church's ministries. Most recently a concentrated effort has been made in a tutoring program for the public high school.

By meeting with the school's principal, permission was granted enthusiastically for us to begin a tutoring program that would pair women with one or two students. Offered as one of the electives in the weekly Women's Ministries Program, the women carpooled to the high school and met with their students for approximately thirty-five minutes. Our providing a nursery and going as an organized group enabled many more women to participate.

The students volunteered for the program and seemed to need encouragement more than heavy academic tutoring. After the students returned to their classes, each session was closed with a prayer time. The experience encouraged some women to tutor for a longer length of time on another day of the week.

God honored the commitment of the women in tremendous ways. By being faithful every week, the school officials and students knew it was *God's* love that motivated the women. Special relationships were made as only God could ordain, and women who had never seen the community before became burdened for the families who lived there to experience God's love and healing in their lives. The women saw answered prayers and a school welcoming their participation.

The only requirement is a willingness to serve God and flexibility in doing so.

Appendix Four

SAMPLE SIGN-UP FORMS FOR WOMEN'S MINISTRIES SERVICE OPPORTUNITIES

WELCOMING NEWCOMERS TO NBC

This ministry consists of simply calling, welcoming, offering information, and answering questions about our church to women who visit.

_____ Yes, I'd like to welcome newcomers.

Name _____ Telephone number _____

_____

_____

THE CRISIS PREGNANCY CENTER

Are you interested in having a direct impact on the fight against abortion? Become a volunteer at the Crisis Pregnancy Center. Volunteers answer the hotline in their home or counsel women who come to the center. They inform them about the truth of abortion and have an opportunity to tell them of God's love for them. Volunteer counselor training is given. CPC also needs baby furnishings and maternity clothes. Contact: (name and number)

_____ I'd like more information before I make a decision

_____ I'd like to investigate

_____ Volunteering as a counselor about 4 hours a week with training (a desperate need currently)

_____ Opening my home to an unwed mother

_____ Donating maternity clothes, infant clothes, equipment

_____ Baby-sitting for the children of volunteers in my home so others can be counselors

Name _____ Telephone number _____

_____

_____

WOMEN'S MINISTRIES BULLETIN BOARD

_____ I would be willing to keep the bulletin board updated and see that it gets properly placed on Tuesday mornings.

Name _____ Telephone number _____

_____

_____

MISSIONS PROJECTS

At the end of each session, the teaching tapes are sent to our women missionaries. Other areas of outreach to our women missionaries will be explored this year.

_____ Yes, I could help prepare and address the tapes for mailing.

_____ Yes, I'd like to be involved in exploring other ways we can encourage our missionaries.

_____ Here's an idea I have _____

_____

Name _____ Telephone number _____

_____

_____

HOSPITAL VISITATION

"I was sick and you visited Me" (Matthew 25:36 AMP). Show the women of (Northwest) the love of Christ by visiting them in the hospital or later at home. Guidelines and helps provided. Contact: (name and number)

_____ Yes, I'd be willing to make hospital visits.
_____ I'd like more information before I decide.
_____ Yes, I'd do this if I could go with another person.

Name _____ Telephone number _____

_____

_____

NEW MOTHER VISITATION

Like babies? Join the team that visits new mothers in the hospital or in their homes. Call it a labor of love and encouragement. Contact: (Name and number)
_____ Yes, this sounds like fun. I'll try it!

Name _____ Telephone number _____

_____

_____

WEST DALLAS MINISTRY

NBC helped found and continues to support the West Dallas Community Church, pastored by Aarvel Wilson. He and his wife, Eletha, not only minister to the community's spiritual needs but reach out in all the areas listed below and *more*. In what area can you help? No experience needed in any area, only a caring heart. Contact: (name and number) or (name and number)

I would like to learn more about and/or become involved in:

_____ Tutoring 1–2 times a week in the 1st, 2nd or 3rd grades at Carver Elementary School.

_____ Tutoring students at Pinkston High School in a room set apart especially for NBC to help them prepare for the TEAMS test to graduate.

_____ Helping call Pinkston High parents when children miss school.

_____ Helping with some of the 32 freshmen at Pinkston involved in the "I Have a Dream" program.

_____ Helping at West Dallas Church once or twice a week with adults and young people to help them pass the GED test.

_____ Doing something of my choice at the Senior Citizens Center, such as setting up and showing one of the many videos from our church library or the *Jesus* film, performing music, helping with a craft, games, or visiting.

_____ Spending time with young mothers who need some knowledge in caring for their babies and basic living skills for themselves.

Name _____ Telephone number _____

_____

_____

HELP IN CHURCH OFFICE

When our church office has special projects or large mailings that could use extra hands, would you come to help and have fellowship with our secretarial staff and other volunteers while stuffing envelopes, etc.?

_____ One day a week. *Which day?* _____

_____ One day a month. *Prefer* _____

_____ Place my name on a list to be called. I'll help when I am available.

Name _____ Telephone number _____

_____

_____

DONATIONS FOR THE CHURCH NURSERY

_____ I can donate good, used children's clothes (birth to 6 years) to be given to (1) our missionary families, (2) our church families, (3) West Dallas Church.

_____ I can make/donate doll clothes.

_____ I can donate doll bedding.

Name _____ Telephone number _____

_____

_____

DALLAS LIFE FOUNDATION

This is a shelter that houses, feeds, and offers clothing to many homeless in Dallas. It is located near Old City Park.

I'd like to know more about:

_____ Leading or helping with a Bible study for women

_____ On Monday evenings _____ During the day

_____ Teaching or helping with a class on caring for and disciplining children from newborn to 6 years

_____ Offering or helping with a craft-type class to foster women-to-women fellowship and encouragement

_____ Arranging or helping with an outing to the zoo or a museum or other free activities for DLF residents

_____ Teaching a 1–4 week class such as cooking for one, cooking in a Crockpot, nutrition

_____ Donating a _____

Name _____ Telephone number _____

_____

_____

Exploring New Ministries

WIDOWS' SUPPORT GROUP

Women who have experienced the loss of their husbands will be able to minister to those who are suffering the same loss. This ministry will be for encouragement and fellowship.

_____ Yes, I would work with other interested women to start this group.

_____ Someone I know who might be interested in this group _____

Name _____ Telephone number _____

_____

_____

MINISTRY TO NURSING HOMES

_____ I would like to be involved in ministering in nursing homes.

_____ I could serve in the following ways:

_____

_____

Name _____ Telephone number _____

_____

_____

ADOPT A GRANDPARENT

A family who is far away from their own parents may wish to reach out to a senior citizen in our body who has no family or who is living far away from his or her family. Both sides could be enriched by these relationships.

_____ Yes, I'd like to participate in Adopt-a-Grandparent

_____ I'd like some family to adopt me as their grandparent

_____ I'd like to help facilitate such a program

Name _____ Telephone number _____

_____

_____

SUPPORT GROUP FOR PARENTS OF CHILDREN WITH SPECIAL NEEDS

(Name) teaches a special Sunday school class at 11:00 on Sunday mornings for children at NBC who have special needs.

_____ I would like to help get such a support group started.

Name _____ Telephone number _____

_____

_____

SUGGESTIONS OR QUESTIONS

_____

_____

_____

_____

_____

_____

_____

_____

Name _____ Telephone number _____

_____

_____

Appendix Five

SAMPLE WOMEN'S MINISTRIES FLYER AND BROCHURES

Variety is an ever developing aspect of the creative ability of women to respond to others and to our culture. The sample brochures and flyer in this appendix show some of the ways to advertise events in the Women's Ministries Program in your church.

- Women's Ministries Saturday Special (flyer), Northwest Bible Church, Dallas, Texas
- Women's Ministries Registration Brochure (2001–2002), Northwest Bible Church, Dallas, Texas
- Women's Ministries Spring Bible Study Brochure (2001), Northwest Bible Church, Dallas, Texas
- Women's Ministries Spring Session Brochure (1992), Northwest Bible Church, Dallas, Texas

Women's Ministries Saturday Special

July Saturday Special
July 11th
Speaker: Alicia McNairy
"Seeking the Wisdom of God"
9:15–2:00 Bring a sack lunch
Nursery by reservations only (Bring lunch for children)

ELECTIVES:

Elective #A Beads Beads Beads
There are lots of fun things you can do with beads. Join us to make button covers and earrings. Then let your imagination run wild. Requires no talent.
Leaders: Pat Mills, Carol Cox   Cost: $6.00

Elective #B Child Rearing
Opportunities for mothers of young children to talk about training, discipline, and problems of rearing children in a biblical manner.
Leader: Norma Kennedy   No Cost

Elective #C Garage Sales
Stretch your decorating dollars by shopping at garage sales and outlets. Share special bargains with the group.
Leader: Jean Ann Bristol   No Cost

Elective #D Rubber Stamping
Come learn the basics of rubber stamping and much, much more. We'll be making birthday cards.
Leader: Suzy Robb   Limit: 15   Cost: $4.00

_____

Name _____ Telephone _____
Elective_____ 2nd Choice _____
Nursery Reservations: Child(ren) _____Age(s) _____

_____

Turn in reservations to the Women's Ministries Office, Northwest Bible Church

Women's Ministries 2001~2002 Registration

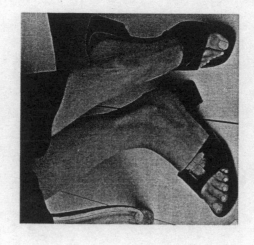

Northwest Bible Church
8505 Douglas Avenue
Dallas, TX 75225

2001~2002 Calendar

- **September 4** Annual Kickoff
- **September 11** Tuesday Bible studies begin
- **September 22** Designing with Confidence
- **October 5-7** Fall Retreat
- **October 11** Heart-to-Heart Kickoff Dinner
- **October 27** Change Your Life Conference-Becky Tirabassi
- **December 8** Christmas Luncheon
- **January 9-30** Personal Profile Series II
- **January 25-26** Intimate Issues Conference
- **March 1-2** Prayer Retreat
- **April 13** The View
- **April 20** Heart-to-Heart Tea
- **April 23** Tuesday Bible studies end
- **June** Summer Series Begins

Women's Ministry
(214) 368-7092, ext. 421

WELCOME

Dear Friend,

Are you looking for just the "right shoe" that fits your spiritual needs? Women's Ministries invites you to try on our " new shoes" designed to help you walk closer to the Lord and connect with other women.

Stop by and see us.
We're looking for you!
Dianne Miller
Minister to Women

Women's Ministries of NBC aims to enable women to intimately know Jesus Christ and make Him known

through diligent prayer, study and application of the Scripture.

through developing and using our gifts in service.

through loving, intergenerational relationships.

WOMEN'S MINISTRIES

Tuesday Bible Studies

A time of worship, teaching and small group discussion in the book of Daniel on Tuesdays beginning September 11th at 9:30 AM and 7:00 PM. Tuesday morning childcare provided. Contact Sara at sbarbee@nbctexas.org.

Heart-to-Heart

Heart to Heart encourages relationships between women from different ages and stages of life. The Kickoff Dinner will be hosted on October 11th and the Tea on April 20th. Contact Margaret at margaret_noblin@msn.com.

MOPS

MOPS (Mothers of Preschoolers) welcomes the community to join this international, new-to-NBC program. MOPS meets every other Friday morning at 9:00, beginning September 7th. Contact Jennifer at JJpharris@msn.com.

Retreats

Our Fall Retreat is October 5-7 with guest speaker Pam Moore. Contact Ginny at gp2tthmas@airmail.net. The Prayer Retreat will be held March 1-2 with special guest Kay Johns. Contact Ann Day at annday@tomellis.com. Advanced registration required for both events.

Christmas Luncheon

The annual Christmas Luncheon will be hosted at NBC on Saturday, December 8th with guest speaker Arlene Pellicane. A special time to celebrate the season with family, neighbors and friends. Contact Amy at awalz@highpointtravel.com.

Personal Profile Series II

Wednesday evenings in January, Dianne and Jeff Lawrence teach how your personal life story affects your relationships and your place in our community. Contact Sara at sbarbee@nbctexas.org.

Someone Cares

For the post-abortion individual experiencing residual grief, this is an outreach to see you fully restored to fellowship with God, and to know that you are forgiven. Contact Beth at elizabethannmckee@hotmail.com.

West Dallas Tutoring

Are you interested in mentoring and tutoring children in grades K-3 in a West Dallas school? If so, contact Polly Urquhart at pnudru1@swbell.net.

For more information, visit www.nbctexas.org/women.

INTEREST FORM

We invite you to complete this form and return it to the Women's Ministry office of NBC or register online at www.nbctexas.org.

Name _____

Address _____

City/Zip _____

Phone _____

Email _____

I am interested in the following women's ministry opportunities:

___ Tuesday morning Bible study
___ Tuesday evening Bible study
___ Heart-to-Heart*
___ MOPS*
___ Fall Retreat*
___ Prayer Retreat*
___ Christmas Luncheon*
___ Personal Profile Series II
___ Someone Cares

Names/Ages of Children:

_____
_____
_____

* Further registration required

204

NORTHWEST BIBLE CHURCH

Women's Ministries
Spring Bible Study

Living by the Power of His Love

Join us for this exciting series on the Book of John. Dianne Miller will lead us as we discover truths that will revolutionize our thinking, living and loving.
CLC Quad A

Tuesday Mornings
9:30 – 11:45 a.m.
Beginning February 6, 2001

Wednesday Evenings
6:15 – 8:00 p.m.
Beginning February 7, 2001

Each session begins with fellowship and Bible Study followed by electives.

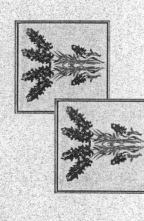

Calendar

February 6, 7	Spring Bible Study Begins
March 13, 14	Spring Break
April 24, 25	Spring Bible Study Ends
June 6	Summer Bible Study Begins

Ministry Opportunities

DTS Food Basket
Leader: Cindy Taylor 214.363.-092
Promiseland Journey
Leader: Nancy Ricker 972.713.6159
Sisters in Touch
Leader: Bette Smyth 214.319.9447
Someone Cares
Leader: Beth McKee 214.363.5396
Uplifters
Leader: Nancy Christy 214.349.2262
West Dallas Tutoring
Leader: Cathy Martin 972.243.3496

But these are written that you may believe that Jesus is the Christ, the Son of God, and that by believing you may have life in his name.

John 20:31

Visitors and Guests are Welcome!

Tuesday Morning Electives

Elective 1: *Bible Study Follow-Up*
Expand your understanding of the Book of John through small group discussion.
Leader: Dianne Miller

Elective 2: *A Beginners Quilt*
Introduces fabric selections, basic cutting, piecing and quilting techniques. Starting with a "rail fence" lap quilt. Requirements: basic sewing skills and access to sewing machine. Cost: $10 book optional and materials
Leader: Lisa Lilley 972.664.1564

Elective 3: *Missionary Prayer*
This group enjoys the blessing of interceding for the ministries and lives of each of NBC's missionaries.
Leader: Polly Urquhart 972.960.0665

Elective 4: *Spiritual Disciplines for Ordinary Women*
How do I grow? What does a spiritually mature person look like? Join us for discussion and application of John Ortberg's book. Cost: $11 for book
Leader: Myra Boynton 214.341.8991

Elective 5: *The Christian Family*
How to establish a Christian home, find models worth copying, learn your responsibility as a wife/mother and more. Leader: Sally Thor 214.692.8000

Elective 6: *Women in Prayer*
Women will share their lives and needs with each other as they pray for each other and the NBC church family.
Leader: Pam Wheatley 972.726.6484

Elective 7: *VBS Help*
Join us as we prepare nametags and crafts for the many children who will attend VBS.
Leader: Karin Roundtree 214.368.7092 ext. 130

Elective 8: *Stimulating Development in Children*
Want to enjoy activities with your kids and contribute to their social, intellectual and language development? Learn how to turn off the electronics and turn on learning and enjoyment.
Leader: Kay Giesecke 214.522.5650

Wednesday Evening Electives

Elective A: *Bible Study Follow-Up*
Expand your understanding of the Book of John through small group discussion.
Leader: Dianne Miller

Elective B: *An Introduction to Photography*
Learn how to get better photos from your point-and-shoot or semi-automatic camera. We'll discuss the elements of composition, equipment, film, hints and tips.
Leader: Mary Burkhead 214.219.4022

Elective C: *Joy of Simplifying Your Life*
This workshop will streamline your soul, goals and activities. It is a continuation of the fall elective by the same name, but newcomers are welcome.
Leader: Peggy Grant 972.732.6950

Elective D: *The Disciple's Life*
Is it really possible to experience His presence daily, hourly? Discover how to experience God's sufficiency and grow in intimacy with Him as you study the classical spiritual disciplines.
Leader: Jan Winebrenner 972.867.1119

Elective E: *The Sacred Romance: Drawing Closer to the Heart of God*
We will be reading and discussing the book, The Sacred Romance, to help us discover and experience a deeper love relationship with God. Cost: $10
Limited to 15
Leader: Joye Baker 214.368.2904

Elective F: *VBS Help*
Join us as we prepare nametags and crafts for the many children who will attend VBS.
Leader: Karin Roundtree 214.368.7092 ext. 130

Elective G: *Ministering to NBC through Prayer*
Gather to praise and petition God on behalf of our church family.
Leader: Kathy Burns 214.373.1702

Elective H: *Ragtime Quilt*
Join us as we make an easy, cuddly, fast, machine quilt. You'll finish in 8 weeks.
Leader: Betty Burkhart 214.826.3745

Registration Form Spring 2001

You may mail (Attn: Women's Ministry) or take this form to the Women's Ministry Office of Northwest Bible Church at 8505 Douglas Avenue, Dallas, TX 75225 or register online at www.nbctexas.org.

Name _____

Address _____

City/Zip _____

Home Phone _____

Email _____

Elective Choice

I will attend ___ Tues. Morning ___ Wed. Evening

1st Choice _____

2nd Choice _____

Tuesday Child Care Registration (Ages 0-5)

Child's Name _____

Child's Birthdate _____

Child's Name _____

Child's Birthdate _____

If you have questions, please call Women's Ministries at 214.368.7092 ext. 170

NORTHWEST BIBLE CHURCH

WOMEN'S MINISTRIES

Spring Session, 1992

God's Power For Our Inadequacy
The Life of Moses

Vickie Kraft
Bible Teacher

Tuesday Morning
March 24-May 12
9:30-12:00 Program
10 minute fellowship break between
Bible Study and Electives
Wednesday Evening March 25-May 13
6:45-8:30 p.m.

WEDNESDAY EVENING

Elective #C Current Issues for the Working Woman

A study based on the book Your Work Matters to God, by William Hendricks and Doug Sherman. Work dominates the landscape of modern life but unless you can connect what you do all day with what you think God wants you to be doing, you will never find ultimate meaning in either your work or your relationship with God. It starts with a certainty that "your work matters to God".
Leader: JoJo White

Elective #D Bible Study Discussion

Please join us for an in-depth study of the Bible lesson. This elective will provide a structured setting for probing of the Scriptures, for applying God's Word, and for keeping each other accountable.
Leader: Bobbi Wignall

Elective #E The Finishing Touch

Do you have any unfinished projects—your needlework or recipe files, photo albums, thank-you notes, etc.? Join other women and pursue your projects while you share, pray, encourage and enjoy each other's company.
Leader: Daphne Emslie

Elective #F Search for Significance

Most everyone yearns to feel worthwhile, but instead of pursuing the typical wrong goals, this class will focus on the biblical approach to finding significance. We will use the workbook by McGee.
Leader: Angela Adams   Limit:10

Elective #G Rubber Stamping

Come and learn the basics of how to use rubber stamps, plus how to emboss, make pop-up cards and other clever techniques. Something new every week.
Leader: Suzy Robb   Material Costs: $10

Spring Session Registration

Name _____

Address _____

City & Zip _____

Phone _____

Church Home _____

Class Choices: *List 2nd and 3rd choice*

_____ Tuesday Morning _____ Wednesday Evening

1st _____

2nd _____

3rd _____

Tuesday Morning Children's Program
Birth through Kindergarten, indicate birthdate
Reservations must be made for childcare

Name _____ Birthdate _____

Name _____ Birthdate _____

Name _____ Birthdate _____

Return to the registration tables or mail to:
Vickie Kraft, Northwest Bible Church,
8505 Douglas, Dallas, 75225.

For Those Attending Bible Study, The Following Groups Are Available ...

Elective #1 Vacation Bible School Workshop

A great way to help with summer VBS-planning, praying, and making nametags and decorations. Helpers of all ages and talents welcome. This year's theme is "Jesus is Our King", and children will be meeting Jesus as they hear the parables.

Leader: Mary Flo Ridley

Elective #2 Rubber Stamping

Come and learn the basics of how to use rubber stamps, plus how to emboss, make pop-up cards and other clever techniques. Something new every week.

Leader: Suzy Robb   *Material Fees: $10*

Elective #3 Homework Assistance at Pinkston High School

If you are interested in missions, but say "Please don't make me go to a foreign country!", come to West Dallas to assist high school students with their homework and prepare them for major exams. No expertise required. Training included in the first session. Carpool from church at 10:45, return by 12:15.

Leader: Joy Beless and Carroll Turpin

Elective #4 Potpourri of Cooking

Join us for a variety of culinary delights, ranging from appetizers to desserts, healthy and gourmet. Enjoy learning how to prepare the specialties of different cooks and enjoy tasting them, too, of course.

Leader: Glad Ramirez   *Cost: $12.00*

Elective #5 Bible Study Discussion

Please join us for an in-depth study of the Bible lesson. This elective will provide a structured setting for probing of the Scriptures, for applying God's Word, and for keeping each other accountable.

Leader: Pat Mooty

Elective #6 The Finishing Touch

Do you have any unfinished projects—needlework or recipe files, photo albums, thank-you notes, etc.? Join other women and pursue your projects while you share, pray, encourage and enjoy each other's company.

Leader: Marlyss Skipwith

Elective #7 Originally Yours

Who says you can't paint shirts like the pros?! We have Cricket by the Creek short sleeve shirts ready for your signature, and if the paint lasts, try your luck on tennis shoes, sunglasses and bathing suit coverups. It's fun, food, fellowship and art.

Leaders: Carol Cox and Pam Nesmith   Cost: $15

Elective #8 Nutrition's Focus

A practical and healthy approach to nutrition including nutrient and energy needs, cholesterol and fat recommendations for children and adults. We'll also discuss guidelines for establishing healthy eating behavior in children and dealing with those picky eaters, low fat cooking, recipes, and eating out.

Leader: Paula Nyman, R.D., L.D.

Elective #9 The Austrian Craft Connection

"We Can Do it!" Perhaps you are not called to foreign missions, but you CAN contribute some crafts and handwork for our missionaries, which they can use in their ministry. Join us for fellowship, fun, craft making and prayer.

Leader: Shirley Rogers

Elective #10 Let's Make a Memory/Tradition

Join us and hear a different speaker each week share their established family memories/traditions concerning the different holidays, family activities, food, decorations and ideas that teach the joy and fun of being part of a Christian family.

Leader: Pat Humphrey

Elective #11 Learn to Teach a Bible Study

A class for those who feel motivated to teach biblical truths to others. We will look at the principles of communication and practice how to deliver a message effectively. Come learn and practice the valuable art of teaching others God's truth.

Leader: Lynna Lawrence   Limit: 10

Elective #A Home Schooling

We will explore the ups/downs and ins/outs of home schooling. This class will be aimed at those considering home schooling for the first time, but anyone interested may come.

Leaders: Beth Pattillo, Bonnie Dettmer

Elective #B Beginning with Christ

This class is for those people interested in a brand new relationship with Christ and those who want the practical steps to living the Christian life, i.e. reading the Bible and praying.

Leader: Sue Farr

More Wednesday Evening
On Reverse Side

208

Appendix Six

SAMPLE HEART-TO-HEART FLYERS AND BROCHURES

With the advent of computers and desktop publishing you have available myriad ways to advertise and organize your program. The following pages are just a few examples from the women at Northwest Bible Church given to stimulate your own thinking and creativity. Each example illustrates a different aspect of the Heart-to-Heart program.

- Introductory Letter
- Profile Sheet
- Matches Structure
- Covenant for Partners
- Steering Committee Responsibilities
- Evaluation Survey
- Brochures
  Introductory brochure, Christ Community Church, Omaha, Nebraska
  Heart-to-Heart Kickoff Dinner, October 11, 2001, Northwest Bible Church, Dallas, Texas
  Heart-to-Heart Kickoff Dinner, October 12, 2000, Northwest Bible Church, Dallas, Texas

September 7, 1998

Dear Heart to Heart Partner,

On behalf of the Heart to Heart Committee, I want to thank you for considering an opportunity to unleash God's power through the women of our church! When we as women are connected through God's Word and prayer, His love leads us to knowing and caring for each other's needs in ways only He can understand. He "Ties Our Heartstrings Together"!

In Titus we are commanded to teach the younger women, and this year we want to extend this commandment from our eldest women down to our youngest babies and toddlers. With this in mind, we offer a variety of matches: <u>Tried and True</u>, the traditional one on one match; <u>Heart to Heart to Heart</u>, an opportunity for group interaction; <u>E-xceptional Heart to Heart</u> designed for encouragement, sharing, and mentoring via E-Mail; and for the Junior and Senior High girls of NBC, <u>Budding Heart to Heart</u> as an introduction to mentoring through prayer commitment. A detailed match structure sheet is included for your information. We hope that the Lord will use these relationships to strengthen friendships and our church community across all generations here at Northwest.

Please take the time to investigate the assortment of options we have to obey the commandment in Titus 2. Not only will it be <u>fun</u>, but it will link the women of Northwest Bible Church supernaturally - allowing God to work within us!

God Bless,

Suzy

Suzy Henson
Chairman, Heart to Heart Committee

1. Check Type of Match Desired

☐ Tried & True
☐ Heart to Heart to Heart
☐ Exceptional Heart to Heart

1998-99 HEART TO HEART
Profile Card

Please fill out all information, use the back or another sheet if necessary!

2. PERSONAL INFORMATION:

NAME:_____

ADDRESS:_____

CITY, STATE, ZIP:_____

PHONE: Best Time to Contact:_____

        Home:_____   Home Fax:_____

        Business:_____   Business Fax:_____

        Cell or Pager:_____   E-Mail Address:_____

Age:_____Birthday:_____Marital Status: S M W D

Profession:_____

Spouse's Name:_____

Children's Name(s) and Age(s):_____
_____

3. NORTHWEST BIBLE CHURCH INFORMATION:

Attended Since:_____Sunday School Class:_____

Will Attend Women's Ministry: Tuesday Morning_____Wednesday Night_____

Will Attend Heart Warmers Elective: Tuesday_____Wednesday:_____

Other Church Activities Involved In:_____
_____

4. TELL US ABOUT YOU!

Please add any other information which will help us match you with a suitable partner. Continue on the back if necessary.

When did you become a believer?_____

Please tell us about your interests, hobbies, talents, desires, needs, hopes and passions!_____
_____

What other Christian activities are you involved in?_____
_____

What time constraints do you have?_____
_____

Why do you want to have a Heart-to-Heart Partner and what are your expectations?_____
_____

What do you have to give to the relationship?_____
_____

Confidential information may be mailed to the Heart-to-Heart Coordinator: Suzy Henson, 5916 Glendora, Dallas, TX 75230.

Heart to Heart
MATCHES STRUCTURE
The Season of Friendship is October through September

Tried and True

One on One matches between a Mary and an Elizabeth, with a monthly get-together and a weekly phone call. Plan to attend the Women's Retreat together and all Heart to Heart functions.

Heart to Heart to Heart

Group matches with one Elizabeth and a group of Marys or two Elizabeths with one or two Marys. This can be multigenerational. Plan to attend the Women's Retreat together and all Heart to Heart functions.

Exceptional Heart to Heart

One on One match for those who are "on-line"! Mentoring & Encouragement handled primarily via E-Mail as often as desired. Monthly get-togethers and attending Heart to Heart functions are highly recommended.

Budding Heart to Heart

One on One matches with a Junior High Girl and a Toddler, with a weekly prayer commitment for the Toddler and a monthly phone call to the Toddler's mother for prayer requests, updates and development. This match is accountable to the Junior High interns.

One on One matches with a Senior High Girl and a Junior High Girl with a weekly prayer commitment and monthly phone call for updates, prayer requests, encouragement, and exchanging scripture. This match is accountable to the Senior High Interns.

Heart to Heart Covenant

Leadership Team's Covenant

We will strive to honor God in our personal lives.

We accept the mandate given in Titus 2: 3-5 and will be in Heart to Heart relationships based firmly on God's Word.

We will faithfully pray, meet, and plan for the Heart to Heart matches and ministry.

We will offer group Heart to Heart activities, a quarterly newsletter, opportunities for follow-up and help with your match, an interactive elective designed for you and your partner, prayer support, and additional resources and services if issues are deeper than a mentoring relationship should provide.

We are available to you throughout your relationship for ideas, suggestions, spiritual guidance, and concerns. Confidentiality will always be honored.

We will prayerfully match Heart to Heart partners using shared interests and life experiences. Above all, we will seek God's leading through His Holy Spirit.

We have formatted these expectations for our Heart to Heart Leadership Team and covenant with God, each other, and you to honor them.

Heart to Heart Partners' Covenant

Strive to honor God in your personal lives.

Accept the mandate given in Titus 2:3-5 and work to build your Heart to Heart relationship on God's Word.

Faithfully keep your commitments to talk to, meet with, and pray for your partner.

Attend and participate in as many Heart to Heart activities as possible (hopefully together).

Share concerns, problems, prayer requests, suggestions, creative ideas, etc. with the Heart to Heart Leadership Team.

Having prayerfully and thoughtfully filled out the Profile Card, accept your Heart to Heart partner joyfully praying for God to use your match for His glory and your edification.

I accept these expectations for my Heart to Heart match and sign my name as a covenant with God, her, and the Heart to Heart Leadership team.

Please take the time to write your expectations for your personal Heart to Heart match in the space below. Sign it, exchange one copy of it with your partner, keep one for yourself and return one copy to your contact person on the Leadership Team.

EXAMPLE

Signed: _____

HEART-TO-HEART

STEERING COMMITTEE RESPONSIBILITY

Support program by:
1. Presenting Heart-to-Heart Program concept to classes or groups.
2. Attending coffees for matching of partners.
3. Supplying breads, fruits etc., for coffees.
4. Attending committee meetings.

ASSISTANTS
1. Arrangeplace for coffees as needed. These can be held at the church or in a home near the church on days when nursery facilities are available.
2. Provide invitations and announcement.
3. Make arrangement with nursery and secure someone to take nursery reservations. (Extend nursery facilities 45 minutes past end of coffee).
4. Get count of those planning to attend and try to even up Junior and Senior partners by calling those who have previously attended but have not made a match.
5. After coffee take names of matched partners.
6. Make list of those that did not match up and specify if they are Junior or Senior partner.

HOSTESS
1. Supplies home and beverage. (Committee members shouldarrive 30 minutes early to assist hostess as needed).

COFFEE
1. Have sign-in(name, address, phone, Junioror Senior partner.)
2. Name tags in two colors- designate one for Junior andone for Senior partner. Colorful sticker could be used to designate those already with a partner.
3. Sharing time initiatedby leader (committee member)presenting two or three questions from which each chooses one to share with group.
4. After group sharing, conceptand commitment of Heart-to-Heart program is presented by committee member.
5. We ask Junior partners to select senior partner to whom they can relate.
6. Mothers with children must pick up children by time arranged with nursery.

COFFEE FOLLOW UP
1. Give copy of list to chairman.
2. Follow-up and meet with chairman and Minister to Womento try to match up those that did not make match.
3. Keep list current as to those who still want to be a part of program

HEART TO HEART
SURVEY

1. Did the Heart to Heart program meet your expectations? Why or why not?_____
   _____
   _____

2. What activities did you and your Heart to Heart partner participate in?_____
   _____

3. Would you participate in the program next year? Why or why not?____
   _____

4. Would you recommend the program to others? Why or why not? _____
   _____

5. How would you improve the Heart to Heart program? Suggests please?
   _____
   _____

6. Was the time frame for the Heart to Heart program (fall through spring) to short, to long or just right? _____
   _____

7. Should the Heart to Heart pairs meet as an entire group more often? _____ If so, what activities would you like to see or recommend?
   _____
   _____

8. Did the Heart to Heart program help you grow as a Christian woman?
   _____

9. Is this a program the church should continue? Why or why not?_____
   _____

OTHER COMMENTS:_____
_____
_____
_____

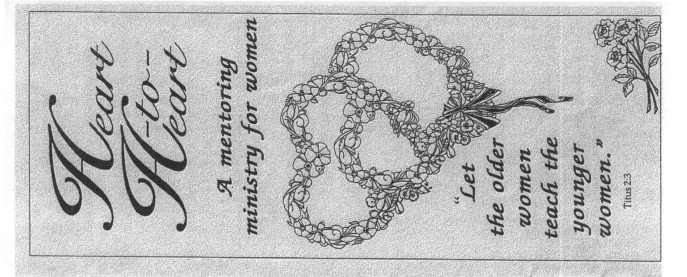

Heart
~to~
Heart

A mentoring ministry for women

"Let the older women teach the younger women."

Titus 2:3

CHRIST COMMUNITY CHURCH
Omaha, Nebraska 68154-2662
402/330-3360

Each of you should look not only to your own interests, but also to the interests of others.

(Philippians 2:4)

Excellence is willing to be wrong;
Perfection is being right.
    Excellence is risk,
        Perfection is fear.
    Excellence is powerful,
Perfection is anger and frustration.
Excellence is spontaneous,
    Perfection is control.
Excellence is accepting,
    Perfection is judgment.
    Excellence is giving,
        Perfection is taking.
Excellence is confident,
    Perfection is doubt.
    Excellence is flowing,
    Perfection is pressure.
    Excellence is journey,
    Perfection is destination.[1]

1. Between Women of God, Donna Otto, Harvest House Publishers

217

What is it?

- God's call for women to open their lives and hearts to the next generation. Share goals, dreams, and your own personal spiritual journeys.

- A mentoring ministry that helps older and younger women develop important, supportive friendships.

- An opportunity for younger women to tap into the reservoir of experience, empathy, maturity and spirituality that older women can often provide.

GUIDELINES

- Make a one-year commitment to the relationship

- Contact each other once a week and meet at least once a month

- Pray for each other regularly

- Do things together (study the Bible, shop, learn a new skill, go to lunch, etc. – partners are free to do what they want as long as they work on developing a Christ-centered relationship.

Who Is It For?

- All women in our church – any age and any level of spiritual maturity

- Older women – in terms of life experience and walk with the Lord, not necessarily chronological age

- Younger women – who may come from broken homes, or are seeking role models who can give them hope and confidence that lifelong marriage is possible, or who need someone near when family lives far away

For more information about this ministry, please call Boots Backens at 493-1146.

How Others Have Responded . . .

"The young women in my world, daughters of my heart, have changed me, rearranged me, and brought a quality of life that I never dreamed possible. They have been the Energizer battery in my life."

"As an older woman, I have experienced the joyful and not so joyful times as a wife, mother, and homemaker. I am able to encourage younger women in these areas from a Christian perspective. However, I gain as well as give. I enjoy the concern and love I've received, and I love their youthful vitality, humor, and enthusiasm for life. It keeps me thinking young!"

"My mentors have helped me find Christ and discover how to live a life that pleases Him. Each one delivered her message differently, and each one was effective."

"I love opportunities to share because I always come out knowing more than when I began. The Lord seems to reveal truth in the midst of Heart-to-Heart sharing. Jesus' command to love one another is uppermost in my walk, and I am hungry to form new relationships that go below the surface. I've learned that giving and receiving are never one-sided and that I need the Body. I look forward to being kept up-to-date by a younger person so I don't get out of touch."

"I want to be of help and encouragement to a young mother, to lend a listening and sympathetic ear, and to share my experiences that might apply to her situation. I want to show her how God has been faithful and led me through every trial and met every need in my life."

"I love talking to my senior! She is always nonjudgmental and gives a calm balance to my life. Her strong faith, evident in every situation, is an encouragement. She is a great role model."

"By watching my senior partner demonstrate strength in the midst of tragedy, I learned great lessons about what it means to trust in God, to rest in God, and to know God."

"I have been exceedingly blessed by the spiritual nurturing I have received from my senior partners. One has taught me how to be joyful regardless of circumstances. Another has modeled unselfish giving. My present partner has encouraged me beyond measure to keep time with my Lord and family at the forefront of my life. I so wish to be a godly woman, and I am grateful for their guidance, availability, and loving care."

When women's unique needs are met through godly role models, the entire church is blessed.

How You Can Get Involved . . .

- Register in the Worship Center lobby August 2-16.
- Complete a profile sheet to assist us in matching you.
- Come to the breakfast on October 10 to meet your Heart-to-Heart partner.

Northwest Bible Church

Heart to Heart...

Ministry weaving the strings of NBC's women together

Save the Date

Heart to Heart Kickoff Dinner

October 11, 2001
6:30–8:30 p.m.

$8.00 per person

RSVP (214) 366-0855
By October 4, 2001

Questions?

Call Margaret Noblin (214) 366-0425 or
E-mail her at margaret_noblin@msn.com

www.nbctexas.org

Please number (with 1 being the most important) the priorities you would like considered as you are matched.

Category	#	Comments
Interests/Hobbies		
Geographic Proximity		
Married/Single		
Parenting skills		
Discipling/Bible study/prayer accountability		
Career experiences/ Leadership skills		
Other		

Any other comments that would help us with your Heart-to-Heart placement?

_____

_____

Would you be willing to help with Heart-to-Heart functions throughout this year?

_____

What is Heart to Heart?

Do you need a friend? Heart to Heart is a program that has been successful in developing, supportive, spiritually focused friendships between older and younger women in our church.

Titus 2:3-5 places the responsibility for teaching and discipling younger women upon the maturing older women. **Women understand Women!** The empathy, trusting in God, and the various life experiences of older women create an enormously powerful reservoir of untapped God-given strength and encouragement for younger women. The Heart-to-Heart Ministry taps this reservoir by pairing older women with younger women in a friendship relationship for one year.

What kind of time commitment does Heart to Heart require?

In order to develop your friendship, partners should get together at least once a month. The length and location of your meetings is entirely up to you. Staying in touch with each other by phone or e-mail between meetings will enhance your relationship.

How can I get involved?

Please take time to pray and then fill out the attached profile card if you would like to commit yourself to this ministry for one year. You may mail (Attn: Women's Ministry) or take this form to the Women's Ministry Office of Northwest Bible Church at 8505 Douglas Ave, Dallas, TX 75225 or bring to the Women's Ministry Table in the CLC.

What are the different kinds of matches?

 ### Tried and True
One-on-one match between a younger woman and an older woman

 ### Group Matches
One or more younger women with one or more older women who meet as a group and/or individually as desired to build relationships among partners

 ### E-mail
Designed to give encouragement through E-mail

 ### Cascading
An older woman develops a relationship with one or more younger women who in turn are matched with one or more younger (than they are) women. The women can meet individually or as a group.

Profile Card

Check type of match
[ ] one to one match
[ ] group match
[ ] email match
[ ] cascading match

Name: _____
Address: _____
Phone: _____
E-mail: _____
Age: _____ Marital status: S M W D
Occupation: _____

Children's names/ages: _____

What are your expectations in regard to your Christian spiritual development?
_____

How did you become interested in participating in Heart to Heart?
_____

How often do you think you could meet with your Heart-to-Heart?
[ ] Weekly
[ ] Every 2 weeks
[ ] Monthly

In your Heart to Heart relationship, do you want a relationship with someone the same age, older or younger?
_____

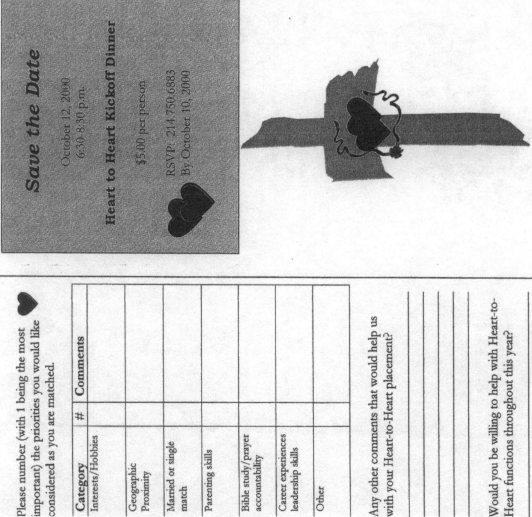

Northwest Bible Church
Heart to Heart Ministry

Weaving Together the Heartstrings of Women

Save the Date

October 12, 2000
6:30-8:30 p.m.

Heart to Heart Kickoff Dinner

$5.00 per person

RSVP: 214.750.6883
By October 10, 2000

Questions?
Call: Suzy Henson 214.750.6883
email: suzyhenson@aol.com
Stacy Rasquinha 972.395.9999

www.nbctexas.org

Please number (with 1 being the most important) the priorities you would like considered as you are matched.

Category	#	Comments
Interests/Hobbies		
Geographic Proximity		
Married or single match		
Parenting skills		
Bible study/prayer accountability		
Career experiences leadership skills		
Other		

Any other comments that would help us with your Heart-to-Heart placement?

Would you be willing to help with Heart-to-Heart functions throughout this year?

What is Heart to Heart?

Do you need a friend? Heart to Heart is a program that has been successful in developing supportive friendships between older and younger women in our church. *Titus* 2:3-5 places the responsibility for teaching and discipling younger women upon the maturing older women. **Women understand Women!** The empathy, trusting in God, the various life experiences of older women create an enormously powerful reservoir of untapped God-given strength and encouragement for younger women. The Heart-to-Heart Ministry taps this reservoir by pairing older women with younger women in a friendship relationship for one year.

What kind of time commitment does Heart to Heart require?

In order to develop your friendship you should get together at least once a month. The length and location of your meetings is entirely up to you. Staying in touch with each other by phone between meetings is a positive help to the relationship.

How can I get involved?

Please take time to pray and then fill out the attached profile card if you would like to commit yourself to this ministry for one year. You may mail (Attn: Women's Ministry) or take this form to the Women's Ministry Office of Northwest Bible Church at 8505 Douglas Ave, Dallas, TX 75225 or bring to the Women's Ministry Table in the CLC on Sunday mornings.

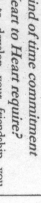

What are the different kinds of matches?

♥ *Tried and True*
One-on-one match between a younger woman and an older woman

♥ *Group Matches*
One or more younger women with one or more older women who meet as a group and/or individually as desired to build relationships among partners

♥ *E-mail*
Designed to give encouragement through email

♥ *Cascading*
An older woman develops a relationship with one or more younger women who in turn are matched with one or more younger (than they are) women

This ministry promotes friendships of love, support and guidance.

Profile Card

Check match desire: [ ] one to one match
[ ] group match
[ ] email match
[ ] cascading match

Name:
Address:
Phone: h   w
email:
Age: Marital status: S M W D
Occupation:
Children's names/ages:

How long has living the Christian life been important to you?

Why did you sign up for Heart to Heart?

How often do you think you could meet with your Heart-to-Heart?
[ ] Weekly
[ ] Every 2 weeks
[ ] Monthly

Which pairing best describes the kind of relationship you would like?
___ Mother/Daughter
___ Grandmother/Granddaughter
___ Sister/Sister
___ Teacher/Learner
___ Friend
___ Mentor
___ Prayer Partner
___ Christian Role Model
___ Accountability Partner
___ Other, explain

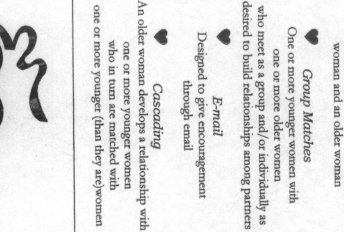

Titus 2:4 Ministries – Real Answers for Today's Women

Contemporary Christian women are facing an array of confusing and conflicting voices about how to live a successful life. To maximize her God-given gifts and design, today's woman needs:

CLARITY With constant exposure to secular feminism and humanism many women are confused, uncertain, and even resentful about their role as unique individuals. Women are greatly enriched by clear, biblical direction on God's loving design and plan for their lives.

SUPPORT As culture continues to break up families and other vital relationships, younger women often have no mature female model to turn to. Titus 2:4 Ministries helps forge new bonds.

MENTORS Younger women still express the desire for role models of Christian womanhood. This is a key role of mothers that contemporary lifestyles have too often crushed. The church and resources like Titus 2:4 Ministries need to rebuild mentoring relationships. The **Heart to Heart** program has been successful in initiating these relationships.

GUIDANCE To many families the professional counselor or therapist has become a key to coping. Churches can supplement these resources by engaging biblically-equipped, mature and godly women in this role.

"Likewise, teach the older woman to be reverent in the way they live, not to be slanderers or addicted to much wine, but to teach what is good. Then they can **train the younger women** to love their husbands and children, to be self-controlled and pure, to be busy at home, to be kind, and to be subject to their husbands, so that no one will malign the word of God." **Titus 2:3-5**

Engaging Needs with Resources to Meet Them

Titus 2:4 Ministries equips mature and godly women to meet the needs of other women in the church.

PURPOSE Our mandate comes from Titus 2:3–5 and our tools are forged from biblical principles that result in fulfilled lives marked by God's joy and freedom.

The need for women to encourage women is not new. It has been a part of God's design for millennia. The first century church learned the model well. Now, with the many challenges of third millennia culture, it is time to return to the God-given foundation for happy and meaningful womanhood.

Sadly, many mature Christian women have turned away from the church for fulfillment. Community and cultural institutions know well the power of the volunteer woman: the church too often does not know how to engage her in meaningful ministry.

The experience, empathy, maturity and spirituality of many of these mature women are enormously rich and powerful reservoirs of untapped, God-gifted strength which the church must learn how to utilize or risk losing them and the generations which follow them.

TOOLS Titus 2:4 Ministries puts tangible, workable tools into the hands of mature women in the church so that they can fulfill their biblical roles. This is done in a variety of ways: CONFERENCES • RETREATS • BOOKS • COUNSEL • CONSULTING

CONTACT US AT: P.O. Box 797566 • Dallas, Texas 75379-7566
972.447.0252 • Titus24women@aol.com

Sɪɴᴄᴇ 1894, Moody Publishers has
been dedicated to equip and motivate
people to advance the cause of Christ by
publishing evangelical Christian literature
and other media for all ages, around the
world. As a ministry of the Moody Bible
Institute of Chicago, proceeds from the
sale of this book help to train the next
generation of Christian leaders.

If we may serve you in any way in your
spiritual journey toward understanding
Christ and the Christian life, please
contact us at www.moodypublishers.com.

*"All Scripture is God-breathed and is useful
for teaching, rebuking, correcting and training in
righteousness, so that the man of God may be
thoroughly equipped for every good work."*
—2 Tɪᴍᴏᴛʜʏ *3:16, 17*

MOODY
PUBLISHERS
THE NAME YOU CAN TRUST